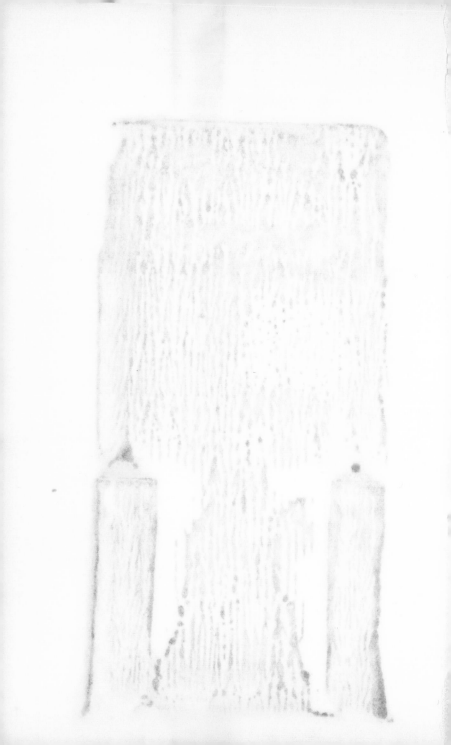

DIMENSIONS OF ACADEMIC FREEDOM

University of Illinois Press

Walter P. Metzger
Sanford H. Kadish
Arthur DeBardeleben
Edward J. Bloustein

Urbana   Chicago   London   1969

DIMENSIONS OF ACADEMIC FREEDOM

Foreword

In the spring of 1968 the College of Law of the University of Illinois sponsored a series of lectures designed to explore the "Dimensions of Academic Freedom." Supported by a grant from the S & H Foundation of the Sperry and Hutchinson Company, the law faculty invited four men—a historian, a university regent, a law professor, and a college president—to visit the university and address the community. The participants brought a diversity of insight as well as experience, and offered those who met with them most thoughtful discussion of the process and problems of academic freedom.

It was felt that the statements presented deserved to be broadcast to an audience larger than that which could be accommodated in the auditorium of the Law Building. A generous contribution of funds by the administration of the University of Illinois made possible the publication of the papers in this volume. For this support and that of the S & H Foundation, for the cooperation of the University of Illinois Press, and for the editorial assistance of Mrs. Zelda Derber and Mrs. Marilee Brukman, Associate Editors of the University of Illinois Law Forum, the law faculty is most grateful. We extend special thanks to our contributors, whose efforts are, after all, the reason for this book.

John H. McCord
Chairman
Lecture Committee

Contents

Academic Freedom in Delocalized Academic Institutions

Walter P. Metzger

The gist of the argument that follows is that the theory of academic freedom as it has been articulated in this country has become, in critical respects, outmoded. By this I do not mean to imply that the value of academic freedom has diminished; it is not only relevant to the modern university, but essential to it—the one grace that institution may not lose without losing everything. A theory of academic freedom, however, goes beyond an affirmation of its value to a description of the forces and conditions that place this desired thing in peril, and a prescription

WALTER P. METZGER. Ph.D. 1950, University of Iowa; Member, Committee A (Academic Freedom and Tenure), American Association of University Professors; Member, Academic Freedom Committee, American Civil Liberties Union; Joint author, *Academic Freedom in the United States* (1955); Professor of History, Columbia University.

1

of the norms and strategies that may offset those specific threats. It is in this latter sense, as a mode of analysis and advice concerning the realities of social power, that I believe the inherited canon has, to a large degree, outlived its day.

One should not suppose that the American theory of academic freedom owes its staleness to senescence. Though it draws on an ancient legacy of assumptions, it did not become crystalized in this country until as late as 1915, when Arthur O. Lovejoy of The Johns Hopkins University, E. R. A. Seligman and John Dewey of Columbia University, and a number of other academic luminaries wrote the *General Report on Academic Freedom and Academic Tenure* for the newly founded American Association of University Professors. To call this report a classic is to comment on its quality, not its venerableness—a document only two generations old hardly qualifies as antique. But a short period in the life span of ideas may constitute a millennium in the time scale of institutions, especially American institutions, which have been known to change at breakneck speeds. What has happened in the half-century since 1915 is that American universities have been remodeled while the ideas once consonant with them have not. The result has been a growing discrepancy between milieu and theory—an ever widening culture lag.

By the lights of 1915, a violation of academic freedom was a crime designed and executed within the confines of the university. Dissident professors were the victims, trustees and administrators were the culprits, the power of dismissal was the weapon, the loss of employment was the wound. Concentrating on this stage and scenario, the authors of the 1915 statement concluded that the key to crime prevention lay in the adoption of regulations that would heighten the security of the office-holder and temper the arbitrariness of the "boss." So persuaded, they persuaded others, and in time these institutional regulations, known as academic tenure and due process, came to be widely adoped if not always faultlessly applied. It should be noted, however, that by defining a violation of academic freedom as something that happens *in* a university, rather than as something that happens *to* a university, these writers ignored a set of issues that had caused their foreign counterparts much concern. Nothing was said in this document about the relations of the academy to state authority. Except for brief allusions to the class obsessions of wealthy donors and the populistic foibles of local legislators, nothing was said about the external enemies of the university, though history made available such impressive candidates as the meddlesome minister of education, the inquisitorial church official, the postal guardian of public morals, the intruding policeman, and the biased judge. Finally, nothing was said about threats to the autonomy of the university that were not, at one and the same time, threats to the livelihood of its members; indeed, it was not even clearly acknowledged that a corporate academic interest, as distinct from an individual academic's interest, existed and had also to be preserved. In short, 1915's criminology (and the criminology operative today—cf. the policing efforts of Committee A of the AAUP) was wise to the ways of the harsh employer, but it lacked a theory and vocabulary for dealing with the outside offender and the nonoccupational offense.

Along with this definition of the crime went a

recommended rule of good behavior: a university, the report declared, should never speak as an official body on matters of doctrine or public policy. In the lengthy history of universities this gospel of institutional restraint had not had many preachers or practitioners. Indeed, there were many more examples of commitment: e.g., the adherence of the continental universities after the Reformation to the confessional preferences of the local rulers, the involvement of Oxford and Cambridge in the dynastic struggles of Tudor England, the proselytizing efforts of the church-built colleges in America prior to the Civil War. The authors of the 1915 statement took aim at this tradition by attacking some of its basic premises: that truth is something to be possessed rather than endlessly discovered; that truth-questions yield to the edicts of institutions rather than to the competitive play of minds. Intellectual inquiry, they insisted, had to be ongoing and individual; organizational fiats defeat it because organizations are mightier than individuals and fiats are inevitably premature. In support of their brief for neutrality they likened the true university to an "intellectual experiment station" where new ideas might safely germinate, to an "inviolable refuge" where men of ideas might safely congregate, and—most simply—to a "home for research." By no stretch of analogy was the modern university to be considered a missionary society, a propaganda agency, an arm of a political party: it was a residence, a hothouse, a sanctuary—the figures of speech were adoring, but they left the university with nothing of substance to proclaim.

How was this no-substance rule to be effectuated; what were the means to this lack of ends? Here our near-yet-distant academic forefathers made another enduring contribution. Conceivably they could have argued, taking a cue from the independent newspaper with its balanced display of editorials, that an academic institution achieves neutrality by appointing men of varying opinions to its faculty. Or they could have argued, with an eye on the renunciative code of conduct common in the military and civil service, that an academic institution achieves neutrality by prohibiting its members from speaking out on public issues, especially on those foreign to their specialities. Significantly, the authors of the AAUP report did not accept either of these possibilities, but instead set forth a formula possibly suggested by the economic market: let the university disown responsibility for everything its members say or publish and then let it permit its members to say and publish what they please. This formula, which was to be made more explicit in later decretals, had obvious advantages over the others. Neutrality by disownment was easier to administer than neutrality by selection, harder to abuse than neutrality by proscription. But it also created a peculiar asymmetry: it asserted, in effect, that professors had the right to express opinions but that their colleges and universities did not.

By including the concept of personal freedom under the rubric of academic freedom, these writers made their doctrine even more asymmetrical. Traditionally, academic freedom had merely offered on-the-job protection: freedom of teaching and research. These, it had been supposed, were the main arenas where professors exhibited special competence and where they deserved a special latitude; beyond lay a terrain of utterance which professors, like any other citizens, were presumed to enter at their own risk. The authors of the 1915 report would not accept such zonal ordinances. Academic freedom, they asserted, protects professors in all of their identities—as teachers, scholars, scientists, citizens, experts, consultants—and on every sort of platform. It applies not to a category of speech but to a category of persons.

What, in the American experience, gave rise to this cluster of pronouncements? A thorough answer to this question would entail an exhaustive history of libertarianism in America—a project which, if I were ever brave enough to tackle, I would never be brave enough to do in haste. But I may, within my boundaries of space and courage, offer up a partial answer—one having to do with the congruence between the ideas of these professional spokesmen and the institutional life they knew.

The first and most important thing to be said about the college or university of 1915 was that it possessed and exercised impressive powers within a demarcated area. This attribute, which I shall call its "localness," derived in part from the clarity of that demarcation. The lands of the college of that period usually made up a contiguous property and were often marked off by fences that kept the students in corral and warned the outsider of the line of trespass. Usually they were located in sequestered regions either on the outskirts of major cities or in the bucolic settings of college towns. Spatially these institutions lived apart, and this apartness contributed to their autonomy.

In addition to acreage and location, style and organization fostered localness. Administratively, with the exception of a shrinking number of ecclesiastically controlled institutions, each unit was entirely discrete, with its own board of regents or trustees, its own executive figure, its own sublieutenancy of deans, its own budget, its own rules and regulations. Legally each was endowed by charter or statute with a vast amount of discretionary authority. Extensive in the management of property, that authority was virtually without limit when it came to the regulation of persons. In 1915 neither outside law nor internal dissonances restrained the exercise of student discipline. It was common in those days for students to live under rules they did not fashion and to be expelled for infractions without a trial. When students asked the courts to intervene they usually were disappointed, the courts generally taking the position that students had, by implied or explicit contract, consigned themselves to the mercies—quasi-parental and therefore tender—of those who had initially let them in. It should not be supposed that students submitted gladly to this regimen. The annals of these institutions disclose too many revels in the springtime, too many rebellions in the fall and winter, to support the view that, uniquely in America, 18 to 22 were the docile years. Yet it is also clear that few in this febrile population challenged the legitimacy of that regimen. Students sought to outfox, not unseat, their elders; they made a game of the rules, but accepted the rules of the game. This kind of popular acquiescence, together with the virtual absence of serious judicial review, gave the academy the appearance of a foreign enclave, ruling indigenous peoples with laws of its own devising, enjoying a kind of extraterritoriality within the larger state.

Of course institutions calling themselves academic came in many different shapes and sizes. The grandest institutions of the period—those that had gathered into their custody the tools of modern scholarship and research—were much more involved with the world around them than colleges that were little more than *écoles*. But the worldliness of the Harvards and Wisconsins did not yet undercut their localness. For one thing, research tools were on the Edison scale of cost: Brookhaven magnitudes were not yet imagined. By means of the usual fund drives and appropriations, these institutions could sustain the cost internally and thus keep control of what their members did and spent. For another thing, the scholars and scientists they assembled were still burdened with heavy academic duties. At this point in time, while there were many teachers who did no research, there were practically no researchers who did not teach—and teach assiduously and regularly. In a much more than *pro forma* sense, men who worked *in* the university also worked *for* the university and were responsive to its interests and requirements.

Even in their transactions with their patrons the colleges and universities of 1915 had a great deal of decisional independence. It is a convention of academic history to deny this, to conclude from their chronic neediness, their perennial courting of the legislatures, their incessant wooing of potential donors, that they were the most obsequious of creatures. But I suspect that those who assert this take as their implicit model of comparison the English university of the nineteenth century, an institution that owed its aplomb and self-reliance to ancient clerical endowments, enormous property holdings, and the privileges of the class it served. Without that invidious comparison, the American college would seem to have been made of sterner stuff. For one thing, the bulk of collegiate instruction was still going on in private institutions which, despite many resemblances to the public ones, had a narrower constituency to account to, and far more discretion in defining that constituency. Some were dependent on very rich patrons, and not the braver for it; still, very often, behind the captains of industry who invested fortunes in universities, there would be a charismatic president who told them how their money should be spent. In the public sector, the whims of the men who held the purse strings had to be catered to more consistently, and presidents of state institutions were often chosen for that capacity. Yet even here the processes of negotiation that took place between legislators and administrators left considerable discretion in local hands. Members of appropriations committees seldom developed the educational expertise needed to initiate novel policies. Far from being sources of innovation, these committees were political arenas where administrators would bargain with their counterparts for public monies and where the essential educational decisions would concern the division of the take. Nor was there much regulation of the system, either in the public or the private areas. Large-scale private philanthropy, though it had worked important reforms in such limited fields as medical education, was not yet a ubiquitous improver; agencies for self-regulation, like the regional accrediting associations, tended to be self-protective bodies, shielding the run-of-the-mill establishment against its fly-by-night competitor. Far less than in railroads or in banking were the firms in academe made to conform to specific standards. And the reason for this is not hard to find. Serving a small segment of the population, not yet central to the economy, taken more seriously for its fun and frolics than for its earnest devotions, the college or university of 1915 was regarded as a public ornament and curiosity, not yet as a public utility.

Above all—and this is what makes the period seem an age of innocence, our own academic *belle époque* —the organs of the central state were not intrusive. For years the federal government had given land to universities without conditions, or had laid down conditions (e.g., the furtherance of agriculture and technology) without imposing very strict controls. In 1915 Washington did not even have an apparatus for dealing systematically with academe. The federal interest in education, which was at that time almost negligible, could be contained in a lowly Bureau of Education whose primary task was to get statistics; the federal interest in (nonagricultural) science, which was even at that time quite considerable, could be met by governmental agencies like the Geological Survey and the Naval Observatory, and did not impinge on the universities. Americans tended to attribute this phenomenon—substantial federal assistance without a significant federal presence—to the genius of their Constitution and their history. Doubtless a literal reading of the Tenth Amendment, plus the hold of Jeffersonian prejudices, did erect barriers to state intrusion. Where such barriers did not exist, as in Great Britain in the nineteenth century, universities felt much more statist pressure. Thus, for all their vaunted independence, Oxford and Cambridge were compelled to submit to extensive changes suggested by a royal commission in the 1870's and enforced by parliamentary decrees. But there was still another explanation, albeit one less visible to contemporaries, for the special state of American affairs. In large part our federal government was undemanding simply because it had no urgent demands to make. A nation that had just entered world politics but had not yet become a world power, that lived in the Edenic security of a miniscule army and a safe frontier, lacked one of the principle motives for intermeddling—the motive of martial necessity. Let that motive be supplied, as it would in a future far more imminent than most Americans in 1915 could foresee, and the central state would not scruple to lay a levy on the spirit of the university, as well as on its faculties and young men. Full recognition of this came in 1918 when, on behalf of a country mobilized and gladiatorial, the Congress transformed every college male into a soldier, every college dormitory into a barracks, every college lawn into a training ground under the aegis of the Secretary of War. The Student Army Training Corps, like the agencies of propaganda filled with scholars, was decried as a folly and an aberration as soon as World War I closed. But at the outbreak of World War II the academic system was once more militarized, and this time the marriage of Mars and Minerva would not only be solemnized but preserved.

It is not very difficult to see why the authors of the 1915 statement on academic freedom ignored the macrocosm of society and concentrated on the smaller campus world. It was there that significant things could happen. A college or university was then no mere appendage of government, no mere component in a great machine. It was a unit of considerable completeness, an agency possessed of powers that were almost governmental in kind. It suggested a checkerboard view of power and a concept of academic freedom that was equally sectioned and discrete.

So much for the general bias of the theory. To account for its specific arguments one has to note another feature of the system: its capacity to generate within each unit an inordinate amount of status strain. This was the period when the academic profession came of age: when it came to think of itself as specialized, competent, and scientific; when it sought to act as mentor to society on a wide range of social issues; when it demanded the deference and the courtesy that befitted these pretensions and that role. It happened, however, that this was also the period when many academic trustees and administrators adopted a style of management that conceded little to these demands. Derived from the views and manners of prerogative-minded business managers, falling between an older authoritarianism with its familial emphasis and a yet-to-come bureaucratism with its codes and forms, the style struck many professors as both overweening and capricious, and in any case hostile to their status claims.

An example of the irritating potential of this new managerial psychology can be found in one of the earliest academic freedom cases investigated by the AAUP. In 1915 the Board of Trustees of the University of Pennsylvania dismissed the economist Scott Nearing on grounds they refused to disclose. (The evidence is all but conclusive that they took exception to his opinions, which were radical then, but not yet Marxist.) In explaining why he did not have to explain, George Wharton Pepper, a prominent trustee of the university, said: "If I am dissatisfied with my secretary, I suppose I would be within my rights in terminating his employment." Was, then, a professor simply a clerk? an amanuensis? The chancellor of Syracuse was willing to concede that he was more than that, that he dealt in some fashion with ideas. Still, this administrator did not believe that the creative function of the professor gave him leave to oppose the man who signed his check. The dismissal of Nearing, Chancellor Day believed, was entirely proper. "That is what would happen to an editorial writer of *The Tribune* if he were to disregard the things for which the paper stands. . . ." Were, then, the trustees of a university, like the publishers of a newspaper, the formal proprietors of the property? The editors of the New York *Times,* in choosing not to go so far, offered their own enlightening treatise on academic relationships in America. As they saw it, the university belonged to the donors, who were its fount of wisdom and ideology *in saecula saeculorum;* the trustees were the agents of the donors, charged with the execution of that immortal claim. Professors? They were simply spoilsports, ever ready, under the academic freedom cover, to ask for privileges they never bought:

Men who through toil and ability have got together enough money to endow universities or professors' chairs do not generally have it in mind that their money should be spent for the dissemination of the dogmas of Socialism or in the teaching of ingenuous youth how to live without work. Yet when Trustees conscientiously endeavor to carry out the purposes of the founder by taking proper measures to prevent misuse of the endowment, we always hear a loud howl about academic freedom.

We see no reason why the upholders of academic freedom in this sense should not establish a university of their own. Let them provide the funds, erect the buildings, lay out the campus, and then make a requisition on the padded cells of Bedlam for their teaching staff. Nobody would interfere with the full freedom of professors; they could teach Socialism and shiftlessness until Doomsday without restraint.

Among the changes wrought by time has been the departure of this kind of liveliness from the editorial pages of the New York *Times*.

Cast in general terms, the report of the AAUP professors did not seem to stoop to rebuttal. Yet these Gothic business doctrines shaped the contours of its major themes. The norm of institutional neutrality was not just an ethicist's abstraction: it was a denial of the proprietary claims of trustees, donors, and their spokesmen. The widening of the zone of academic freedom was not simply a reflex of libertarianism: it was an effort to reduce the sphere in which philistine administrators could take action. And the notion that men were in conflict with their organizations—and that this conflict drew the battle lines of freedom—stemmed only in part from an individualistic ethos: it also expressed the viewpoint of a profession whose institutional existence offered too meager status gains. For all its transcendent qualities, the 1915 report was a tract developed for its times.

The times, I submit, have changed. Not everywhere, not in all respects. A small denominational college may still look as it looked in 1915. A major university may still be living off the precedents set long ago. Here and there a donor may still wish to establish an ideology in the course of establishing a schoolroom, or a trustee may still be tempted to utter the platitude of possession. But at the height where one loses particulars and gains synopsis one can see enormous transformations. Of these, one of the most important has been the flow of decisional power from authorities on the campus to those resident outside. Richer, larger, more complex than ever before, the typical modern institution of higher learning is less self-directive than ever before. It has become, to coin a word, "delocalized," with consequences we are just beginning to perceive.

Delocalization has not been a single process but a congeries of processes, all working in the same direction and achieving a common end. The engulfing of many universities by the central city, with the result that everything that we do in the way of land use becomes imbued with political implications and ensnarled in municipal law, is one delocalizing process. The growth of bureaucratized philanthropy as a principle source of academic innovation, the subordination of the judgment of admissions officers to legislative judgments concerning civil rights, the involvement of universities in social welfare and thus with clients it can serve but not control, may be considered others. And so too may the integration of public higher education, the assault on the principle of extraterritoriality, and the enlargement of federal influence due to federal sponsorship of research. These latter processes are so important, both in affecting the character of academic institutions and the viability of the academic freedom theory, that I should like to examine each in some detail.

In 1915 only two states attempted to coordinate the activities of their tax-supported institutions of higher learning. By 1965 only nine states let their state university, land-grant colleges, technical institutes, and teachers' colleges go their separate ways. The trend, moreover, has not only been toward greater coordination but also toward higher degrees of integration. By 1965 as many as fifteen states had given superordinate public bodies the power to alter and create new schools by plan. SUNY, the gigantic State University of New York, was established in 1949 to take charge of forty-six existing public institutions and to set up as many new ones as its over-all blueprint would prescribe. By current reckoning the California Master Plan brings seventy-six junior colleges, eighteen state colleges, and a nine-campus university under the sway of dovetailing central bodies. In the coordinated systems the power of central bodies may be limited to reviewing budgets and programs initiated by the institutions themselves. In the more integrated systems the off-campus boards of control may make decisions on capital investment and tuition levels, architectural design and new site locations, entrance requirements and degree capacities, while the on-campus boards and administrations may make decisions on how those decisions will be carried out. These vertical and horizontal combinations of plants in similar and diverse lines, these unequal allocations of power between the central office and the local branch, this division of territorial markets state by state, make the integrated academic organization and the modern business corporation seem very much alike, if not of kin. And these resemblances are not lost on the faculties they appoint. If we are employed by the educational duplicate of General Motors or United States Steel, some of them seem to be saying, let us be responsive to that reality: let us elect a single bargaining agent to match the collective strength of management; let us fight for our economic interests without the constraints of a service ethos; let us, if need be, strike. Localized institutions tended to generate professional resentment, but delocalized institutions seem to eviscerate professional élan.

The rationalization of public higher education proceeds from three demands that are made upon it: (1) that it accommodate vast enrollments; (2) that it stimulate economic enterprise; (3) that it accomplish both objectives at something less than crushing public cost. These very demands speak eloquently of the new importance that has come to be attached to this activity. So high is the putative correlation between income earned and degree awarded that a college education has become compulsory, not by the edict of law but by the mandate of ambition. So close is the symbiosis of productive industry on the knowledge industry, so glaring is the cheek-by-jowl abutment of technological parks and college greens, that the advertised presence of a campus has become, next to tax abatements, a primary lure to new investment. Private higher education has grown as a consequence of these connections, but public higher education has grown much faster, so that today it enrolls almost two-thirds of all academic students, and is much more heavily subsidized, receiving $100 in tax money for every $35 its private competitors receive in gifts. With the change in the public-private balance, the old popular affection for the small-scale venturer has given way to a quest for tax economies, and the alleged efficiencies of central planning is urged successfully even in staid legislative halls. What had once been regarded as a mere propaedeutic enterprise has thus become, in the course of time, a key to the life chances of everyone, an object of urgent public policy, and a stimulant to the GNP. New layers of relevance have been added; but in the process the old attribute of localness has been stripped away.

The assault on extraterritoriality—the second delocalizing process—engages another set of forces, at work both in the private and public sectors, both on the campuses and beyond. On the campuses the assault is being mounted by a new generation of student radicals: white revolutionaries and Negro militants, advocates of more effective student power, persons lonely in their alienations or drawn into dissentient subcultures—the varied student cadres that distinguish the convulsive present from the prankish and catatonic past. Each group has its own visions and motivations, as can be seen from the instability of their alliances; and none is yet numerically dominant in any student body in the land. But they are increasingly becoming a powerful, pace-setting minority and they share, amid all their differences, a common animus against the discipline which their predecessors did not oppose. Different groups issue different challenges to that discipline. Advocates of student power dispute the validity of rules that are made for but not by the student client; theirs is a constitutional challenge aimed, as are all the challenges of emergent classes, at the habit and principle of exclusion. Partisans of the New Left break the rules to change the

policies these rules facilitate; theirs is a tactical challenge aimed, as are all radical challenges, at the going
morality of ends and means. At times these challenges
overreach their mark. The breaking of certain rules
may mean the disruption of the operations of the
university, which may require the intercession of
police forces and the use of violence on a massive
scale. The end of this chain of consequences is a
greater loss of internal authority than any may have
anticipated or approved. The surrender of the administration to the harsh protectorship of policemen is
often more costly to its authority than the precipitat-
ing student offense. On the other hand, only the most
Sorelian of student radicals could delight in all aspects
of this denouement: the substitution of military for
civilian options, the traumatization of students by
police attack, the devolution of a community based
on shared assumptions into a community nakedly
based on force. Of late, the politics of confrontation
has found another way to exceed its immediate object.
Students engaged in coercive protest have come to insist that amnesty be granted before they will agree to
relent. For those who reject the legitimacy of the
guardians and who wish to stay to do battle yet another day, this demand serves practical and symbolic
purposes. But amnesty wrested from the institution
may not always bring total forgiveness: violations involving trespass or vandalism may result in criminal
arrests. Where the institution is the sole complainant,
it may influence the disposition of these cases; but it
may find it hard to convince the courts to dismiss
the charges when it has surrendered the means to protect itself. The natural effect of amnesty, granted
under duress, is thus to displace the disciplinary

power from the universities to the civil courts. Whether courts or universities act more justly is a question one need not resolve. It is clear, however, that they do act differently, the one being more interested in behaviors, the other in underlying intentions; the one just beginning to grant academic freedom legal status, the other having long made this the value it cherishes above all. But the thrust of modern student politics is to give the temporal rather than the spiritual authority a legitimate judicial role.

Meanwhile, forces outside the university have been working to constrain academic discipline when it *is* applied. Starting in 1961, the federal courts have been deciding that the disciplinary actions of officials in publicly supported colleges and universities must adhere to the due process standards of the Fourteenth Amendment of the Constitution. Whether the officials of private institutions must adjust their conduct to these standards is not, at the moment, certain; but it is highly probable that they will one day be made to do so or suffer reversal in the courts. One may note that the cases setting the legal precedent involved the interests of Negro students who had been punished for participating in sit-ins by administrators of Negro colleges yielding to the pressures of Southern whites. Clearly the judicial concern for student rights was inspired by a judicial concern for civil rights and not by purely academic considerations. Here again, the college, in acquiring new social significance, has lost a measure of its old autonomy. But here one may be permitted the conclusion that, on balance, justice gained.

I come finally to the last delocalizing tendency: the growing involvement of the federal government

with the affairs and fortunes of academe. This is perhaps not the order or the language that the most pas-
sionate critics of that involvement would prefer. But
the virtue in saving it till last is that we may then perceive it not as something *sui generis* but as part of a
broader development; and the virtue in using the word
"delocalizing" when a more accusative vocabulary is
at hand is that we can avoid the dubious imputation
of Pentagon plotting, power elitism, establishment co-
option, and the like. Nevertheless, after this dispas-
sionate preface, I hasten to admit that I believe the
issue now before us is of burning importance. The
advent of a formidable central state—harnessed almost without limit for a world struggle apparently
without end, richer than any other benefactor by
virtue of the federal income tax resource, able to seek
solutions to any social problem, if need be, by pur-
chasing compliance with the cure—is a momentous
event in the life of our universities. Such a behemoth,
as it draws close, cannot help but siphon authority
from other agencies. In part, but only in part, the
speed and volume of the drain from the universities
can be measured by the increase in its assistance. In
1964 federal contributions to higher learning totaled
$1.5 billion. Though this came to only one-tenth of
the total funds received, it constituted, because of its
distribution, a large percentage of the incomes of the
major places—83 per cent of Cal Tech's, 81 per cent
of MIT's, 75 per cent of Princeton's. For home reference, it may be noted that Columbia, third among
recipients, got $51,000,000, an intake that amounted
to almost half of that year's operating budget, while
the University of Illinois, then sixth in order, got
$44,000,000, a smaller part of its total budget but a

not inconsiderable sum. By 1966 the federal contribution had doubled and the federal share of total contributions had risen to approximately one-fifth. In that year the largesse was a little more evenly distributed, but the major institutions were even more glaringly beholden to the generosity of the central state.

It is in the "how" as well as in the "how much" that we locate the delocalizing pressure. During and after World War II, academic scientists high in government and governmental and military officials high on science hit on two devices for channeling federal funds to universities. One was the project grant or contract, which a faculty member negotiates with the granting agency with minimal involvement by his university; the other was the specialized research center, which the university operates for the agency, sometimes without the participation of any faculty member. These devices are supposed to confer a variety of social and scientific benefits. It is claimed that the distant granting agency, with its advisory panels of distinguished scientists, is more likely to rate applicants on their merits than are members of a department when they judge their own. It is claimed that the separation of federal subsidy from federal employment helps preserve individual research initiative, since an academic scientist is free, as a governmental scientist is not, to pursue the project of his own desire. And it is claimed that the funds allotted under these formulas make possible the purchase of scientific apparatus which would otherwise be lost to the academy in the expensive space and atomic age. It is tempting to investigate these claims, to ask whether personal, institutional, or regional loyalties never tincture the judgments of reviewing panels, whether certain kinds of extravagantly priced equipment—like accelerators with ever increasing BEVs—deserve the national priority they have been given, whether freedom of choice is not subtly constrained by the workings of the well-known principle that a man need not marry for money, he may simply seek out the company of wealthy women and marry one of them for love. But these are not the questions before us: what is pertinent is that these devices rob the university of autonomy, the one by making it a bystander in the fostering and reward of its members' talents, the other by making it a kind of subcontractor, dispensing someone else's cash to attain someone else's objectives. Here one might add a quantitative footnote: today, from two-thirds to three-quarters of all money expended on academic research comes from the federal giver through these circumventive routes.

"Washington," notes Clark Kerr, in his study of the "multiversity," the delocalized institution unsurpassed, "did not waste its money on the second-rate." Did it make what was first-rate even better? Looking at the institutional breeding places of the greatest scientific advances of the last two decades, Kerr concludes that the federal research effort did give existing excellences an added gloss. But on the evidence he himself musters, a more pessimistic conclusion might be formed. Taking what is given without question and doing what is asked for by the gift, the front-rank university tends to find itself rich but troubled, powerful in its impact on the nation but weak in the control of its own affairs. It falls prey to what Kerr refers to as "imbalances": the dominance of science over the humanities, the dominance of research over teaching, the dominance of graduate interests over undergraduate concerns. It takes on an ever increasing number of those whom Kerr refers to as "unfaculty": scholars who are added to the staff to assist externally aided projects. Set to the sponsored task but performing no other service to the institution, never eligible for tenure no matter how often contracts are renewed, this new academic breed lives at the periphery of the profession. Fifty years ago only a relatively small group of graduate students, serving as assistants to the senior faculty, was in as marginal a position. Since then, the ranks of this subaltern force have grown, to take care of the burden of instruction that the increased number of students has created and that a research-minded faculty will not assume. In the leading universities these two anomalous groups—the teacher who is still a student and the researcher who is not a teacher—make up a very large part of the total academic work force. With enrichment, then, has come a new diminishment: an increase in the number of appointees who are in but not of the university, sharing in its tasks but not its perquisites, existing under the predestinarian doctrine (so alien to professional doctrine) that good works can never assure election.

A full estimate of the losses incident to gains must include the acceptance of secrecy and deceit, not as adventitious vices but as part of the academic way of life. Federal support for military research must bear a part of the responsibility for the institutionalizing of shady tactics. The aim of military research is to secure time advantages against the enemy; often, to secure these time advantages, it is necessary to prevent premature disclosures; frequently, to prevent disclosures, it is necessary to test the loyalty of participants, limit access to facilities, guard the research records, or control what appears in print. With the Pentagon no less interested in quality than the National Science Foundation or the National Institutes of Health, it was inevitable that funds for the necrophilic sciences, as well as funds for the healing and heuristic arts, would flow to the better universities. But federal support for military research does not account for all the slyness and covertness that afflicts modern academic life. Only a small part of federal support is avowedly military (in 1966, of the total sum supplied by the granting agencies, only 10 per cent went to academia from the Department of Defense). If the secretiveness of warrior organizations accounts for something, the enfeeblement of academic organizations accounts for more. A high susceptiveness to deception was built into the very flabbiness of the grant arrangement. Almost any agency out to promote an unpleasant mission can find a pretext for lodging it in the university, to acquire gilt by association. Federal undercover agents find it easier to carry on their impostures amid the para-academic members of a research project than amid the faculties at large. Above all, universities involved in the project system developed a trained incapacity to look suspiciously at their gift horses, if indeed they looked at all. Thus it happened at Michigan State University that a program for training policemen for Vietnam, set up by a mission-minded agency without close monitorship by the university, was infiltrated by agents of the CIA. The structure, if it did not require hugger-muggery, was certainly not well made to prevent it. And thus it happened that the same surreptitious body gave secret subsidies to a variety of academic enterprises, ranging from area study institutes to international conferences; once inserted, trickery by government became routine.

This is not to say that trickery by government does not exist on the campus in other forms. Modes of underhandedness have long been associated with law enforcement: viz., the policeman posing as a student, the student doubling as a policeman, the government employer asking teachers to snitch on their students and peers. Especially prominent in "Red scare" periods, these forms of deception are not uncommon in the current period, when drugs take precedence over dogmas as items on the list of search. But these tricks have the capacity to outrage professors in almost all institutions where they are practiced. The secret subsidies of the CIA, by contrast, seem to be a good deal less inflaming. For a decade or so they went undetected, though not without the collaboration of a good many professors and administrators in the know. When some of these were uncovered (largely by left-wing student muckrakers), they did cause a stir in certain faculties. Still, it is almost certain that the taint has not been removed from certain projects and that administrative and professional winking goes on. As late as 1964 Clark Kerr could maintain that the federal grant procedure was "fully within academic traditions." Since the CIA revelations, the academic mood has probably not been so complaisant. Yet it is doubtful that many members of the profession would think it wise to change the title of their book from *The Uses of the University* to *How the University Has Been Used*.

How to account for the difference in responses? Simply to say that one form of police penetration serves to enrich professors while the other may serve to chastise them puts the matter of self-interest much too crudely. It would be, I think, both more subtle and more accurate to say that no process of delocalization, unless it threatens the well-being of professors, is presumed to violate academic freedom; and that without a violation of academic freedom, no insult to the university causes broad alarm. In fact, by the tests which the inherited creed imposes, some of the trends I have spoken of seem to have strengthened academic freedom. Ideological dismissals have become rare to the point of being oddities in the larger delocalized institutions. This is all the more impressive because outspoken opposition to war in wartime, which had always been subject to academic penalties, has been allowed to flourish in these places. Furthermore, with very few verified exceptions, the governmental granting agencies have not discriminated against opponents of governmental policies. Not only in crimes, but also in crime prevention, the current period seems to improve upon the past. Tenure (for those eligible to receive it) is at least as safe in integrated public systems as in any other. Academic due process has, if anything, become more rigorous and more codified as the scattered *gemeinschafts* of before merge into centralized *gesellschafts*. Federal-grant universities, with their congeries of projects, are less likely to get domineering presidents (they are lucky to get presidents able and alert enough to keep track of all that is going on). Less privileged colleges and universities, hoping for federal assistance, are less likely to prescribe religious or other doctrines (this is one reason why certain Catholic institutions are moving toward lay boards of control and even toward the norm of neutrality). For renowned professors the new order is particularly

comfortable and protective. If they have greater lev-
erage in bargaining with their institutions, they may
thank the federal grantor for adding to their other
marketable assets the value of a movable money prize.
The flow of perquisites from Washington dissolves
their reliance on the local paymaster, while the tenure
granted by alma mater prevents their subservience to
the outside source. Status satisfactions only dreamed
of may now in actuality be possessed. The autonomy
and integrity of universities? These heavenly things
on earth are not contained in this philosophy.

This is hardly the place to write an academic freedom theory that would meet this day's demands. All
I can do is sketch out certain areas where changes in
the reigning wisdom would do us good. I ask you to
take this as a prolegomenon; a theoretical and practical formulation of the academic ethics we require
must await another Lovejoy or Dewey, distilling sa-
lient ideas from new institutional experiences.

At the top of the list of credos ripe for change I
would put the view that a crime against academic
freedom is a crime against an academic person's rights.
In relevant doctrine it may still be that; but it may
also be an attack on academic integrity, sustained by
the university as a whole. It should be the name we
give to the intrusion of lock-and-key research into an
ostensibly open enterprise. It should be the name we
give to the acts of secret agentry that turn academic
scholars into stooges and their friends and disciples
into dupes. It should be the name we give to each new
chicanery as it is invented. We had no word to describe the recent efforts of the State Department to
place their employees on the faculties of universities,

the better to defend our foreign policy. With a revised academic freedom creed, we would.

Next I would part with the notion that curbs on administrative power answer all of academic freedom's needs. They answer only part of its needs; the other and equally essential instrument is effective academic government. It was well understood by the makers of our Constitution that freedom could be jeopardized by the weakness, as well as the tyranny, of officials. Even so strong a supporter of checks and balances as James Madison saw the need for a powerful president to protect the interests of the nation, especially in its relations with foreign states. The modern university, in no less precarious contact with its environment, should make use of this political wisdom. What this means in practical terms is not that professors should be less secure—the tenure of the federal judiciary was not thought to bear adversely on the energy of the national Chief Executive—but that administrators should be better served. They should have a higher density of competent assistance (it is a shibboleth that administrations are overstaffed—they are undersupplied with ministerial talent, though they may be very well stocked with scribes). They should have powers commensurate with the task of protecting the interests of the university (this would mean greater control over research projects, and less or no involvement with federal research centers). But they should not be left to work alone. The notion that governments govern best whose members participate the least had questionable support in the eighteenth century; in a day when people both within and outside the polity insist on shaping actions that affect them, such a notion would

fail all opinion tests. Nor is this the only reason why
governing responsibilities should be shared, and
shared in the widest manner. The crisis of delocalization requires all those who caused it to help resolve it,
including faculties who had used the institution as a
base for career advantage, and students who had used
the institution as a target of political attack. As for
the risks incurred by the investiture of students, particularly radical students, a word of prudential com-
fort may suffice: it is the outsider, not the insider, who
tends to assail the given world.

In the quest for relevant doctrine, I would also take
issue with the notion that the only respectable university is a politically neutral university. It may not be
easy to reconceive this notion. The norm of institutional neutrality has rolled through our synapses so
often we hardly ever challenge it with thought.
Therein lies the problem: applied unthinkingly to
every issue, it loses its value as a norm and becomes a
recipe for paralysis. One illustration may make this
clear. The Selective Service Administration recently
decreed that college students would be deferred if
they achieved a certain grade-ranking or passed a
certain standardized test. In other words, instead of
classifying by status (all college students), it classified
by status and performance (only *good* college students), and fixed the criterion of judgment. To grasp
the implications of this procedure one need only ask
what the consequences would have been if the draft
authorities had decided to defer not all women but
only *good* women, not all husbands but only *good*
husbands, not all workers in essential industries but
only *good* workers in essential industries. In academic

no less than in conjugal and economic matters, privacy and autonomy are threatened when virtue is not its own but the state's reward. The academy, however, took little corporate action to defend its corporate rights. Proposals for institutional resistance (say by not ranking students or sending in the grades) were usually defeated by the argument that such acts would be politically unneutral, signifying institutional opposition to the draft or the war in Vietnam. This ritualistic application of the neutrality principle resulted from a failure to distinguish between essentially political questions and essentially educational questions having political implications. A theory adequate for our times would have to emphasize that distinction. It would have to reserve the norm of institutional neutrality for questions of the former sort and for them alone. For questions of the latter sort, and I believe the class-rank issue falls squarely within this category, it would formulate a different norm—a norm of institutional regulation, under which things central to the academy could be dealt with by the academy and not passed to other powers by default. Some questions would fall on or near the borderlines and raise jurisdictional dilemmas. But many more would fall to one side or another once the theoretical line was drawn. Thus, whether the state should build an arsenal of secret weapons would plainly be a political question; on this, for reasons that were given long ago and have never lost their validity, the university should be mute. But whether classified research, under state support, should be permitted on the campus would plainly be an academic question; on this, for different reasons, the university should be heard. To assert a normative choice is to reject the radical view that the university must always be political or consent to the evils of society, and the traditionalist view that the university must always be neutral or succumb to the divisiveness of society. Neither argues potently that the university must be independent, and act or not act as its needs demand.

Even if theories were remade, many pressures to delocalize would continue. To ask that the academy come to grips with these is to ask it to formulate counter-policies in apparent conflict with its needs. Delocalization is in part a product of the growing importance of the university: no one could realistically suggest that it retreat to its older insignificance. Delocalization is in part an answer to the financial exigencies of the university: it would be difficult to demand an autonomy that required enormous dollar sacrifices. Moreover, certain delocalizing forces serve as a counter to the overreach of others: large universities in consolidated public systems may squeeze a measure of autonomy from the fact that they can draw on federal subsidies as well as on state appropriations. Nevertheless, some measure of localness can be restored in ways neither retreatist nor impoverishing. The breaking up of large public configurations into smaller subregional complexes might be a step in this direction. The use of collaborative techniques like the sharing of faculties among independent colleges might be another. The diversion of federal aid into student loans, on a scale large enough to let client fees bear the major burden of client costs; the increase in federal aid in the form of institutional lump-sum payments; the decrease in federal aid for big science under academic auspices (other auspices might handle it as well)—all might reinvigorate local power. The localist need not be contemptuous of the rationalizer or believe that he is living in a cost-free system. He need only insist that rationalizations be really rational and that, in the building and rebuilding of systems, costs of every kind be assayed.

The Strike
and the Professoriat

Sanford H. Kadish

The professorial strike and the forms
of unionization based upon its use are rapidly develop-
ing into a major challenge to our traditional academic ways. Events of the last several years leave no
doubt of it.[1]

In December 1965 St. John's University summarily
discharged twenty-two faculty members and gave notice to eleven others that their contracts would not be

[1] When not otherwise stated, the accounts of the strikes described come from the files of the Washington office of the
American Association of University Professors.

SANFORD H. KADISH. B.S.S. 1942, City College of New
York; LL.B. 1948, Columbia University; Chairman, Committee A (Academic Freedom and Tenure), and Member, National Council and Executive Committee, American Association
of University Professors; Contributing author, *Freedom and
Order in the University* (1966); Professor of Law, University
of California, Berkeley.

renewed. This unprecedented purge followed a long period of simmering strife involving in important part the efforts of the American Federation of Teachers (the AFT) to represent the faculty. The following month over fifty faculty members responded by striking—the first major strike in American higher education.[2] Even at this late date the outcome at St. John's is unclear. The school has continued to operate and the released teachers have not been reappointed. But the incident called dramatic attention to the issue of the professorial strike. The American Association of University Proessors (the AAUP), which itself formally condemned St. John's in vigorous terms and placed its name on its list of censured institutions, nevertheless announced through its Executive Committee that the strike was not "an appropriate mechanism for resolving academic controversies or violations of academic principles and standards." [3] This, in turn, proved to be the beginning of an institutional soul-searching on the issue which is still going on within the AAUP.[4]

In the spring of 1967 a popular assistant professor of moral theology at Catholic University in the District of Columbia was given notice of nonrenewal. The reason was widely believed to be his theological liberalism, and large numbers of faculty joined their students in a boycott which lasted for three days and

[2] *See generally* SCIMECCA & DAMIANO, CRISIS AT ST. JOHN'S: STRIKE AND RESOLUTION ON THE CATHOLIC CAMPUS (1968).
[3] 52 A.A.U.P. BULL. 230 (1966).
[4] 53 A.A.U.P. BULL. 121 (1967). A Special Joint Committee on Representation, Bargaining, and Sanctions (of which the author is a member) has formulated a proposed position paper on "Faculty Participation in Strikes." This has now been approved by the Council and is published in the Summer 1968 issue of the *Bulletin*.

ended in a clear victory for the strikers. The professor's contract was renewed, a new acting rector was appointed who reported to the press that he would have joined the strike if he had been a member of the faculty, and active discussions commenced looking toward enlargement of the role of the faculty in governing the university.[5]

In November 1966 sizable numbers of teaching assistants at Berkeley, principally members of the American Federation of Teachers, declined to meet their classes in sympathy with a student boycott protesting the use of outside police and internal discipline against students who obstructed Navy recruiting on the campus.[6] The Board of Regents responded with a resolution announcing that henceforth faculty and teaching assistants who participated in a strike in order to disrupt university activities would be subject to discharge or other sanctions.[7] The debate was joined by the acting president, who interpreted the resolution as merely identifying one cause that might, depending on all the relevant circumstances, warrant some disciplinary action; and by the academic senate, one of whose committees concluded that while irresponsible use of the strike could impair academic freedom of others, it could not be ruled out arbitrarily.[8]

At San Francisco State College the faculty's academic senate voted to take "collective action, including strike, if necessary" if the Board of Trustees adhered to its announced unilateral policy of mandatory discipline of students and faculty found guilty of dis-

[5] Chronicle of Higher Education, May 3, 1967. For an account of the incident *see* Pierce, Beyond One Man, Catholic University, April 17-24, 1967 (mimeo 1967).
[6] 15 CALIF. UNIV. BULL. Dec. 12, 1966.
[7] *Id.*
[8] *Id.* May 1, 1967.

rupting the campus by force or violence.[9] Also at San Francisco State, and at five other California state college campuses as well, a majority of the faculty who voted in a recent election voted in favor of being represented by an exclusive bargaining agent prepared to apply sanctions to obtain economic support for the faculties.[10]

Chicago's public junior colleges, among half a dozen two-year colleges which have accepted collective bargaining, were the scene of AFT strikes in the winter 1966 term, which resulted in a new contract with improved pay and teaching loads.[11] And on April 2, 1968, Chicago's two state colleges were struck and picketed to enforce a faculty demand for collective bargaining.[12]

At the start of the 1966-67 school year 90 per cent of the faculty of the Henry Ford Community College at Flint, Michigan, struck for two and a half weeks to enforce their collective bargaining demands. And at Highland Park Community College, also in Michigan, a twenty-day strike in September 1967 ended with the professors' ratification of a collective bargaining contract.

[9] Chronicle of Higher Education, Dec. 21, 1967.
[10] Ad Hoc Committee on Collective Bargaining of the Academic Senate, California State Colleges, Issues and Answers on Collective Bargaining (1967). *See also* Larsen, *"Collective Bargaining" Issues in the California State Colleges*, 53 A.A.U.P. BULL. 217 (1967). The question voted on was: "The faculty should elect an exclusive bargaining agent from those faculty organizations which are prepared to recommend and apply sanctions in efforts to secure adequate economic support for the goals of the faculties and which are willing to place their names on the election ballot."
[11] Brann, *Unionizing the Academies*, NEW REPUBLIC, Feb. 25, 1967, at 10.
[12] Chicago Tribune, April 4, 1968, §1, at 20, col. 5.

Two years ago campus pressures mounted for stoppages of university teaching to protest the war in Vietnam, only to be turned aside by the ingenious improvisation of "teach-ins" during nonteaching periods of the day and night. And in March of this year some 100 faculty members of Columbia University canceled classes to accommodate a one-day student boycott in protest against the draft and the war in Vietnam.[13]

Now this recital is not designed to persuade you that professorial strikes are breaking out all over or that their legitimacy is the central issue of higher education. But neither are these events isolated incidents. If I read the signs right, we are in for more of the same in the years ahead. Why, after all these years, should we now quite suddenly be faced with these issues? What's happening? Three things, chiefly, I think.

First, there has been an increasing demand for economic returns by those in higher education. As has been rightly pointed out, it is not that we professors have been and now are so exploited that the lid finally threatens to blow off. It is rather that rapidly rising economic returns, brought on by the favorable professorial market and other factors, plus the spectacle of other professions and occupations improving their economic position at a far faster rate than professors, have sharpened the pressures for a fairer share of the national product.

Second, there is the remarkable expansion of higher education to include new groups of institutions—such as junior and community colleges and full-fledged state universities which shortly before were normal schools or agricultural colleges. In many of these places the

[13] N.Y. Times, March 14, 1968, at 45, col. 5.

self-imposed restraints of the academic tradition are much less firmly rooted and receive little support from faculty or administration. Far too many of them are run much as they were before their rechristening as universities—as places of employment dominated by business-minded administrators in the interest of turning out a product they, the managers, deem saleable. The label doesn't change the reality. But it does produce the harvest of hypocrisy—a bitterness of cynicism in those offered the words without the substance of the professional tradition, a cynicism which corrupts academic values themselves as well as the honesty of those who invoke them.

Finally, and of major importance, I think, is the growing claim for the legitimacy of self-assertion by those convinced that their just claims have been denied. We saw the claim dramatically made in the cause of Negro civil rights as it moved from massive self-help to constitutional rights to acts of civil disobedience and, occasionally, to the use of force and disorder in our cities. We see it made in the varieties of mass protest against the draft and the war in Vietnam—in card-burnings, in draft resistance, in marches, in teach-ins. And we see it on our campuses in student uprisings against felt university injustices.

Now the academic or professorial strike—by which I mean the concerted withdrawal of faculty services as a means of pressure or publicity to attain a desired end—raises many issues, and I do not plan to deal with all of them. First, I shall not deal with unionization of professors as such, although it will not be possible to skirt that issue entirely.[14] Second, I want to put aside

[14] It is clear that one cannot talk about the strike wholly apart from the challenge of academic unionization. They have

the question of what the law should be with respect to the academic strike. So far as strikes in the private university sector are concerned, I take it few would support a legislative prohibition. Such laws don't exist today anywhere I know about and they are so foreign to our ethos of freedom of the citizen in noncritical occupations that no one has seriously presented the proposal. So far as strikes in the public sector are concerned, there is plainly no case for special limitations on public university employees as distinguished from other public employees. As for the general issue of restrictions on strikes by public employees, it has received more than its share of attention and I do not propose to deal with it here. Rather, the issue I want to pose is not what we should by law be prevented from doing, but the more fundamental question of what we should do and what we should not do. Naturally, I speak for myself and neither the American Association of University Professors nor any other organization in which I hold office can fairly be held for my sins.

To ask questions of what professors should and should not do invites consideration of our ideals and our special conception of our work and our commitments. What has been the traditional statement of the

both been thrown up together by similar influences and to some extent the strike is the tail which goes with the hide of unionization and collective bargaining. But it is not necessarily so. Unions can and have eschewed the strike weapon. Laws governing public employees often sanction unionization and collective bargaining, but proscribe the strike. And strikes of some kinds can and have occurred independently of unionization as such. And while there is much overlap in the kinds of considerations relevant to an assessment of unions and strikes, the overlap is not complete.

professorial ideal and what relation does it have to the reality we face?

In our dreamy moments we professors like to imagine ourselves as a simple and loosely formed autonomous community of scholars pursuing knowledge as our fancy dictates and sharing what we know with those who want to learn and can. It's a fantasy, of course. There are pockets of higher education here and there which approximate it. But by and large it's a far different world we live in and we know it.

Universities tend to be highly organized and bureaucratic with a group of managers in positions of ultimate authority. The structure has far more the look of a business organization than that of a learned community. There is no single, embracing community of scholars, but an agglomeration of experts in specialized and diversified fields each with their own separate communities.[15] We work for a living like everyone else and paychecks and fringe benefits toll for us too. There are lots of us pursuing knowledge at these places, certainly. Sometimes the pursuit takes the form of a man, his books, and his inspiration. But very often it is quite different. We work on reports or studies commissioned by government, industry, or big foundations. We assemble in teams to carry on large-scale projects, with the lines laid out in advance. We push ourselves on, necks outstretched for the dangling carrot of tenure, promotion, or prestige. We teach, of course. But we teach a structured curriculum, not whatever we fancy. We spend countless hours inspecting and appraising our students and stamping their

[15] *See* Clark, *Organizational Adaptation to Professionals,* in VOLMER & MILLS, PROFESSIONALIZATION 288 (1966).

records with marks of quality. Many of us administer teaching rather than teach—casting our wisdom for fifty-minute intervals into vast and anonymous caverns of indifference, leaving to aspiring juniors the task of probing live minds. Our students? They are out there all right, in force. Some want to learn, at least in the beginning. But then there are the numerous unfortunates for whom a college education is a necessary evil, a pause before their adult lives begin, a painful ceremony of initiation required by the cult of mass higher education.

All this is true, and more. And yet the ideal of the community of scholars persists. We refuse to give it up. You may conclude that this has been one of the things wrong with us. I rather think it has been the saving of us. For the notion is not just a myth. It is also an ideology. University life has been buffeted around and pulled out of shape by new demands and new influences—no more so than many other social institutions in our changing world, but no less so either. What the ideal provides—even as it is more or less contradicted by reality—is a set of values and commitments which enable us to understand better the force and significance of the bewildering challenges we face. It affords a standard for determining what we can adapt to and what we cannot. The principle of freedom in the academy, for example, we struggle to preserve as our life's blood. Bigness and mechanization we know we have to live with. Mass higher education we perceive in many ways as an ideal superior to our own, and we try to make the adjustments as best we can.

I am not suggesting that the ideal of the community of scholars is a fully formed account of what we aspire to. It is more a suggestion than a description of an ideal. Nor do I suggest that even fleshed out in all its implications it provides an instant guide for distinguishing between those new influences which present challenges to stay contemporary and relevant and those which present mortal threats to our integrity as professors. Estimations of this kind require scrutiny both of ourselves, our ideals and the means of their realization, and the nature of the new influences in all their complexity. This is a tall order, particularly for as recent a development as the professorial strike, but it's what I would like to make a try at now. I intend to proceed first, by considering the ideals of our profession against the background of professionalism in general, and second, by considering what is involved in strikes of various kinds and their implications for those ideals. Finally, I want to comment upon the considerations which should guide university administrations in responding to professorial strikes. In short, then, my subjects are the professoriat, the strike, and the administration, in that order.

To speak of the ideals of the university professor with respect to his work brings us inevitably to the general concept of professionalism. I tremble at introducing that word. It invites the worst kind of logomachy, especially since professionalism is so often invoked as a weapon—as a way of attracting prestige and superiority when used about one's own work and a way of telling someone else that he shouldn't do something we don't want him to do when used about his. But it's a danger that can't be avoided. And it's safer to face it openly than to permit it to slink around disguised in improvised synonyms.

Actually, there is a fair amount of agreement among

the sociologists on what it connotes which is generally
harmonious with its usual usage.[16] Professionalism
represents a particular set of beliefs, ideas, and convictions concerning the conditions under which one's
work is, or should be, performed. This set of ideas
centers principally around three conceptions—that of
specialized expertise, of autonomy, and of service.

A condition of professionalism is that specialized
expertise, knowledge, or competence is necessary for
carrying out the allotted tasks. Moreover, only those
who have received this competence through prolonged
education or training administered by qualified professionals are regarded as eligible to carry on the work.
There is disagreement on how much and what kind
of specialized competence is needed to fulfill this condition of professionalism, but this need not detain us.

Autonomy in exercising that competence is an important ideal of professionalism. The professional himself must have final responsibility, though with advice
and consultation among colleagues, to determine how
his work is to be done—what problems should be
dealt with and how, what values should be striven
for, what the criteria of distinction are. And this
autonomy extends to the admission of others into the
professional ranks as well as to the work done.

Finally, there is the ideal of service, which Professor
Wilensky rightly puts as "the pivot around which the

[16] The principal sources from which the following description
is derived are Wilensky, *The Professionalization of Everyone?* 70 AM. J. SOC. 137 (1964); KORNHAUSER, SCIENTISTS
IN INDUSTRY (1962); Marshall, *The Recent History of Professionalism in Relation to Social Structure and Social Policy,*
in SOCIOLOGY AT THE CROSSROADS (1963); VOLMER & MILLS,
supra note 14.

moral claim to professional status revolves." [17] Restricting practitioners to those who meet the standards of competence and education set by the incumbents and insisting upon self-determination concerning all phases of the work are, after all, claims which could be plausibly attributed to self-interest. As such they achieve no more ethical compulsiveness than the claim of a steam-fitter to a higher wage. But it is central to the character of the ideal of professionalism that these demands flow from a moral claim. And that claim is that proper service to the public in the delicate and important area within the professional's competence requires them. Where a service is of vital importance to society and where it requires a high degree of specialized education and training, as well as the subtle intangibles of good judgment, it follows that a necessary condition for its proper rendering is that the entire matter be left completely in the hands of those who possess these qualifications. No hospital administrator, for example, can instruct a physician in the diagnosing or treating of the latter's patient. But the ideal of service not only gives moral support to these claims, it also imposes responsibilities. Thus, central to the professional's conception of his work is dedication to excellence and reliability in the service he provides. A professional earns his livelihood at his work, but the service he provides to other people comes first; and in any conflict between personal or commercial profit and the interests of those he serves, the latter prevails. His relation is fiduciary rather than commercial.

Turning to the university professor as professional,

[17] Wilensky, *supra* note 16, at 140.

it will be observed that the community of scholars image suggests the special professional attributes of his role. His special competence is in the advancement of knowledge and understanding within the discipline of his training and its dissemination through writing and through instruction of the young. Along with law, the clergy, and medicine, his is one of the oldest of the professions. The ideals of service which animate his work consist of the disinterested search for truth and the education of the citizen as well as the training of the professionals of the future—services of indisputable, central value for any civilized society. In his professional role he is the preserver and cultivator of the uses of reason.

The claim for autonomy within his community rests firmly on this service ideal. Like other professionals the highly specialized character of his calling disqualifies others from making the principal judgments about how he should carry on his scholarship and his instruction. Standards and performance must reside in the judgment of the scholarly community if the judgment is to be reliably made. There is in addition another reason for autonomy of particular applicability to the professorial profession. It is that the social value of the service of research and education is substantially diminished to the extent that considerations other than the disinterested and objective pursuit of truth by the scholar are permitted to affect his work. For others to direct him in what or how to study and teach risks not only the misjudgment of the unqualified, but the distortion of those with special interests, whether they be administrative convenience, prejudice, or social acceptability—interests to which the pursuit of knowledge is particularly and acutely vulnerable. In short, academic freedom as well as special competence support the moral claim of the professor to autonomy.[18]

But university professors are employees by definition who render their service through the intermediary of a university which assembles them and their students and furnishes the facilities for their work. Unlike the prototypical professionals—lawyers and doctors—they are not free-lance and totally independent in their relationships with those they serve. Does this fact preclude realization of the professional ideals of autonomy and service? I would think plainly not. As pointed out by Professor Kornhauser, the ministry and university teaching are two of the most venerable of the professions and in neither was independent practice ever important. Moreover, as far back as 1870 in the United States there were twice as many salaried professionals as there were self-employed ones; and today professional people are employed in increasing numbers in industry, government, and elsewhere.[19]

This is not to say, of course, that the organizational context is not a formidable threat to professional values. Indeed, it, plus the pull of the professional's personal self-interests (about which I will have more to say in a moment), constitute two of the most pervasive pressures toward depreciating professional

[18] *Cf.* Clark, *supra* note 15, at 286: "Academic man is a special kind of professional man, a type characterized by a particularly high need for autonomy. To be innovative, to be critical of established ways, these are the commitments of the academy and the impulses of scientific and scholarly roles that press for unusual autonomy."

[19] KORNHAUSER, *supra* note 16, at 4-5. *See* Hall, *Professionalization and Bureaucratization,* 33 AM. Soc. REV. 92 (1965).

norms. But this threat of bureaucratizing the profession may be met by modes of accommodation and adaptation acceptable to the organization and the professional. In other organizational contexts finding these modes is difficult and elusive. In the university, where the conflict has the longest tradition, these modes have been more effectively worked out than in any other context. I do not say adopted fully, though in the greater universities they have been. I say worked out. And this has happened primarily because the conflicts between the professionals and the organization have not been central and constitutional, as in the case, for example, of scientists employed by industry. After all, while a business exists to sell its products or service for profit, not to advance science and technology, what does a university exist for if not to foster and facilitate the professional objectives of its professors—the advancement and dissemination of knowledge? This commonality of the service ideal has helped in infusing professionalism among the university managers, in professionalizing the bureaucracy rather than the other way around.

Helped only, of course. After close involvement with the AAUP and with a number of universities, I should be among the last to find all sweetness and light in the relations between the faculty and university bureaucracies. Administrators usually are ex-professors, but as in other walks of life it's the role that makes the man. Administration tends readily to be regarded, by administrators, as an end in itself rather than a means of furthering the work of professors and students. This happens particularly as administrations become larger, more complex and embracing, as they have in multi-campus systems. Moreover, authority is not always accompanied with the restraint that comes of a perception of one's limited competence. Indeed, power and humility are the oil and water of the social world. And the pressures of public acceptability and happy conformity are hard for administrators to resist. Finally, the administrators themselves are the servants of governing boards usually composed of men with marginal associations with the world of higher education. The private boards are heavily influenced by alumni and donors and *their* ideas of what a university should be like. The public boards serve designedly as the means of public control and influence over universities, introducing constant pressure to make university activities acceptable to the values and expectations of the electorate and its representatives, not to mention the press.

Still, as I have said, partly as a result of the long tradition of professors in universities and partly as a result of the basic commonality of objectives, modes of accommodation have been evolved. The model has been most elegantly set out in a Task Force Report of the American Association for Higher Education, entitled *Faculty Participation in Academic Governance,* and in a *Joint Statement on Government of Colleges and Universities* by the AAUP, the American Council on Education, and the Association of Governing Boards of Universities and Colleges. Essentially the model is built upon the concept of shared authority in which the faculty and administration participate in influence and decision-making. In some issues the voice of the faculty is predominant by nature of its special knowledge and competence and the imperative of academic freedom; for example, in admission, curriculum, methods of instruction and research, degree requirements, appointments, promotions, tenure, dismissal. In areas in which the administration has a functional advantage it has the primary voice; for example, in providing over-all leadership to the diverse constituency of the university, in coordinating the activities of the component parts of the institution, in planning and initiating changes or new programs, and in assuring high standards in departments and divisions, in business management. Even in these matters, however, participation is joint and the mode of resolution of differences within the university is predominately information-sharing and appeals to reason, with the organized faculty voice taking the form of an academic senate as an integral and internal element of the university structure.

This model, with all its implications, exists nowhere perfectly. But it has tended to be the mode of rapprochement between bureaucracy and professionalism in institutions of higher education to which faculties have traditionally aspired. And certainly at our more distinguished and pace-setting institutions it is invariably the operational model, though, needless to say, working with varying degrees of effectiveness.

So much for the professoriat. Now what of the strike? To what extent do academic strikes threaten commitment to and realization of the university professor's ideals of professionalism? I think they do in a variety of ways and I want now to say why. But in so doing I hope I will not be understood as making a case against all strikes in all circumstances. For the moment my object is simply to draw attention to the important considerations disfavoring the strike which derive from the role of professor as professional. I shall have more to say afterwards on the circumstances which qualify the application of these considerations and on the considerations which point the other way.

Of course there are a variety of strikes differing in the nature of their objectives, the time, place, and manner of their calling, and in other ways. But to start let us consider the kind of strike which is being urged upon professors by the American Federation of Teachers as a standard policy—the economic strike as a final effort to prevail on issues of wages and working conditions when collective bargaining reaches impasse. Let me identify five professional values which are imperiled by strikes of this kind: *the service ideal; the moral basis of professional claims; the commitment to shared and cooperative decision-making; the commitment to reason; and the pursuit of distinction.*

The Service Ideal. Professors don't live by ideals alone, either. Their employee status makes them no less dependent on their salary because they are professionals; and if concern with economic returns and better working conditions were held to be unprofessional, only the clergy—and not all of them—would qualify. But the strike on the industrial model as a means of furthering personal self-interest is something else again. For what is entailed is the calculated interference with the flow of the product or service in which one's protagonist has a strong interest, in order to compel him to accept one's terms. The industrial worker at best stops, or at least curtails, the production or sale of goods by withholding his services in concert with others to the detriment of the economic position of the employer, and thereby provides him with a further incentive to grant what the workers seek. What happens when similar strikes are transferred to the university setting is plain enough. The professor brings education, and its attendant activities, to a halt in order to win concessions from administrators, boards, or legislators; and he does so despite the fact that the provision of the service of education and research is central to his professional commitments.

Now it would be implausible to make a parallel between campus strikes and strikes in essential services, like hospitals or transportation. A few more holidays in the academic calendar create some inconvenience to students and others—more or less depending upon the duration of the strike. But it produces nothing like the hardship of withholding hospital services or stopping the means of transporation. And with ingenuity one can often make good the loss to some extent—by extending the term or making up classes or giving out class assignments. But even where serious and irreparable injury is not done, what the economic strike amounts to is that the professor holds his services ransom for his own benefit. And what further adds to its inappropriateness is the way in which pressure is brought. The shutting down of the university poses no direct economic threat to the administration or the governing board or, in the case of a public university, to the state. The pressure on these groups is the pressure that comes from their accountability for providing the services of the university and the public's expectation that they will meet it. Yet providing the services of the university is a pivotal element of the professor's professionalism. The irony of the economic strike is that it operates through the professors' cutting off the service that both they and the governing boards are responsible for providing on the premise that the boards will yield before the professors do to the pressures to continue that service.

This isn't all there is to be said, obviously. The interest of the university and that of its professors are mutual and not antagonistic. Higher salaries help stave off raids and permit more effective recruiting; they avoid the need for professors to divert their energies into other income-producing activity and they avoid the kind of bitterness and resentment which hinder excellence and devotion. And reduced teaching loads are plainly conducive to better teaching and research. Moreover, governing boards and legislatures have their responsibilities too, and these include not only keeping the hotel open but maintaining the conditions of university life which permit its goals to be achieved, one of which surely is a fairly treated and not an exploited faculty. The injustice of exploitation is doubly acute when the victims are constrained by professional commitments to eschew the defenses available to other employees. For these and other reasons professors may legitimately assert what can be taken to be their economic self-interest in a variety of ways. But the unprofessionalism of the strike remains notwithstanding, for the reasons I tried to suggest.

The Moral Basis of Professional Claims. What is involved in the regularized use of the strike in a collective bargaining relationship—not entirely but in important part—is shifting the basis of professional claims from common commitment and moral entitlement to the play of power in a competitive context. The move from academic senates to collective bargaining backed by the strike is a move to the marketplace. And the spirit of the marketplace is that you're entitled to what you can exact and what you can exact is what you're entitled to. To paraphrase the language of the recent Foote Report on University Governance at Berkeley [20] used in reference to student-administration wrangling, the institutionalization of the collective bargaining strike "obscure[s] the special character of a university, by regarding it much as one does any other pluralistic society populated by diverse interest groups and lacking a common commitment to anything more than the bargaining process itself."

Now I hope I have already made sufficiently clear that I am aware that there are in fact diverse interest groups on a campus and that some of the attributes of a pluralistic society are invariably present. This is hardly to say, however, that it is desirable to surrender to those tendencies; still less to augment them by adoption of the trench warfare of the collective bargaining strike and a reduction of faculty claims from the basis of common commitment to that of the play of power.

Take, for example, the claim to autonomy. As I tried to point out earlier, insistence upon independence in planning, performing, and judging work may be regarded principally as either a demand in the employee interest or a claim resting on the requirements of the effective rendering of the services and on its high social importance. What gives the professor's claim to autonomy its moral legitimacy and persuasiveness in the latter sense is his primary commitment to the service of research and education. To the extent that the professor is prepared to subordinate

[20] Report of the Study Commission on University Governance, The Culture of the University: Governance and Education 10 (Univ. of Calif., Berkeley, 1968).

this service ideal to his employee self-interest and to relegate the determination of what he is to be accorded to the play of power in a competitive relationship he has compromised the moral legitimacy of his claim. And the same may be said for other claims, such as the claim to academic freedom.

The Commitment to Shared and Cooperative Decision-Making. The next danger is closely related to that just described. I have in mind the potential destructiveness of the collective bargaining strike to cooperative and shared decision-making between the faculty and the administration and governing board of the university. For what is imperiled by such action is the system of university government which holds the greatest promise for the effective progress of the main business of research and education. In many essential respects decisions taken by the administration in American universities in those matters within its special competence make as necessary a contribution to research and education as the decisions the faculty makes within its sphere. And administrative decisions often have an acutely direct bearing upon the faculty's own professional contributions. In a word, there is in fact a closely meshed interdependence between the university's faculty and its administrators, which indeed provides the rationale of shared decision-making authority.

I would think that the injection of the collective bargaining strike, both in threat and in fact, might prove a formidable obstacle to that salutary pattern of governance. Annual contract time could become annual battle time with the community divided between the faculty and the administrators and each side assigning its men to their battle stations. The strategy naturally impelled is to get as much as you can from the other side with a minimum of loss to your own. Exaggerated claims and overstated positions become the currency of compromise. At the worst, high emotion and distrust are the by-products. I don't say all this must necessarily be. Quite possibly a union of professors negotiating with university administrators, even against the backdrop of a strike threat, would produce an atmosphere different from the industrial counterpart. But situational pressures have their own logic and momentum and it would be surprising if something of this atmosphere were not created. And one could reasonably expect that this embattled and adversary spirit of divisiveness and competition in place of unity and common commitment would infect as well the pattern of relationships during the academic year as the multifarious problems of academic life arise for resolution, whether they be curricular issues, creation of new teaching positions or departments, or broad educational planning and emphasis.

The Commitment to Reason. As university professors we are charged preeminently and consitutionally with the advancement and instruction in the uses of reason. More so than any other group in the community. This entails many things, but at least it entails commitment to noncoercive argument and persuasion, and skepticism of self-interested judgments. To an important extent the strike is inconsistent with such commitments.

I do not want to say that anything more than the presentation of facts and the development of logical inferences in muted conversational tones is an abandonment of reason. Controversial ideas, particularly where they are put to support claims being made of another, must be expected to be put in ways most likely to secure their acceptance. This may often require the appeal to emotion, to other groups in the community whose opinion is important to those we want to persuade, to lobbying and other political arts. Even some kinds of demonstrations designed to marshal and to demonstrate mass support are not necessarily outlaw to reason where rival claims are in contest. A strike is all of these things, to be sure, but it is also something more. I am not ready to mark out the line between aggressive persuasion and coercion, but I submit that a strike is far from the gray margin. In its essential import it entails inflicting and sustaining some injury on another until he concedes what you want—economic injury to the employer in the case of an industrial strike, and the injury of abating the educational processes which the administration and governing board are ultimately accountable for in the case of the academic strike. This, I think, *is* outlaw to the professorial commitment to reason and argument, however acceptable it may be in the competitive world of business and industrial relations. It is, therefore, an injury to ourselves. But it should be said that it also is an injury to our students, whom we cannot escape instructing when we act as professors. When we depart from the methods of reason for ourselves to get what we want, we cannot help conveying a lesson for them when their wants are not satisfied.

There is another point which may not be overlooked. The strike not only forsakes reason in conception. In the strategy of its execution it appeals to sentiments of solidarity calling for the subordination of individualized judgment. A picket line in effect is not simply an invitation to appraise a grievance. It is a signal to join regardless of one's judgment on the merits at the risk of open and notorious disloyalty to the group.

The Pursuit of Distinction. Effective collective action, such as a strike, requires mass support and this is attainable over the long run by appealing to mass interest. This entails a constant quest for political solidarity even as against academic principle and practices; for example, protection of the employee against discharge or nonrenewal whenever his case is arguable, or sometimes even when it is not; salary increases controlled by automatic formulas rather than by professional judgments of merit; timidness in the face of damaging or irresponsible behavior by faculty members. In a word, the push for distinction tends to be redirected, simply by the dynamics of collective action, toward solidarity, with consequent loss to the educational enterprise. "Solidarity Forever" would be a more stirring and indigenous strain than "Gaudeamus igitur," but less suitable for campuses than for union halls.

I have to this point been addressing the economic strike in the context of collective bargaining. Let me now consider another kind of strike which differs in that its occurrence is independent of collective bargaining and its predominant purpose is not the furthering of self-interest but the furthering of some academic interest, such as academic freedom, shared government, or educational policy. The St. John's or Catholic University strikes are cases in point. What damage to professional commitments are there here?

The analysis must be different from that of the collective bargaining economic strike. The interest asserted is not principally the economic self-interest of the professor, but rather those very ideals and practices of academic life which are indispensable for the effective rendering of education and research—academic freedom, professorial autonomy in matters necessarily committed to them. Further, what is entailed is not an institutionalized dichotomy between staff and managers mediated by a regularized use of force or its threat, but an *ad hoc* response to what is believed to be a radical and intolerable departure from essential standards of academic life. Nonetheless there is a difficulty and it arises from the fact that the strike, for this or any other purpose, constitutes a subordination of reason and persuasion to the use of coercion, usually founded upon a wholly self-made judgment of the rightness of one's cause. I have already described the damage this entails for professorial commitments in discussing the economic collective bargaining strike. The same is true for the academic interest strike, notwithstanding the difference in the aims sought.

The point may perhaps more clearly be made by comparing the measures for redressing academic injuries which have become respectable, such as censure by the AAUP or withdrawal of accreditation, or its threat, by the relevant accrediting agency. Both are forms of pressure, but they differ in several relevant respects. First, these latter sanctions operate directly against the offending institution rather than through the abatement of student education. To be sure, students may ultimately be adversely affected by either sanction, and substantially so. But the sanction is directed to the source of the offense and the harmful consequences follow from the wound the university has inflicted upon itself, whether it be by marring the atmosphere of academic freedom or falling below minimum educational standards. Censure and withdrawal of accreditation are the verification of these self-inflicted wounds, not their infliction. Second, the processes of invoking the sanction are markedly different. The decision to strike in protest is generally made at mass meetings by those personally and profoundly interested, usually quickly and in heat. This is in sharp contrast to the patient exploration of the facts, the hearing of all sides, and the final decision made by noninterested parties which characterize censure by the AAUP or withdrawal of accreditation by an accrediting agency. The latter are not inconsistent with the commitment to reason, truth, and disinterestedness. The former tends to be. No one who has spent years, as I have, reviewing and judging alleged violations of academic freedom and tenure can fail to be impressed by how complicated the circumstances can be or how readily one can fall into error in the facts or in final judgment. What at first blush appear to the interested complainants (and also to groups on the faculty who have heard only part of the story) to be outrages at times turn out to be quite otherwise after investigating committees have explored the circumstances and interviewed the interested parties. Sometimes the case is without merit. Sometimes it is closely balanced. Sometimes the blame is shared by faculty as well as administration. Not always, of course. But often enough to raise grave reservations over the resort to the strike, with its consequent damage, whenever a sizable group on the campus feels that an academic wrong has been done.

I have talked about the economic-interest strike

and the academic interest strike. A word now about what may be called the political interest strike—a concerted refusal to meet classes, for example, as a means of dramatizing a deeply felt disagreement with some political policy, such as the war in Vietnam. Here the direct injury to students is slight since by definition these are symbolic, short-lived protests. And since the university administration is a bystander rather than a protagonist the considerations deriving from faculty-administration government of the university are not the same as they are with the other kinds of strikes. But the fatal danger to university life which they pose is their potential politicization of the enterprise of learning. They entail an official, professorial view of a point of political concern and thereby tend to convert one of the few institutions in society dedicated to objectivity and sober and skeptical inquiry into a partisan arena for political demonstrations. This by itself could have troubling and unsettling effects on the free pursuit of scholarship and education. What augments the danger is that it involves a self-destruction of the main barrier to the political and social thrusts of the outside community, the barrier of the principled neutrality of universities as institutions.

As individuals we have our viewpoints on political and social issues of our times. As professors, in that role, we do not. Our only corporate commitment is to academic freedom and autonomy within the university because these are the indispensable conditions for our work, for learning and the pursuit of truth. This is the posture of neutrality which affords maximum protection against the winds of political controversy, which allows us to claim just entitlement to public and governmental support regardless of what political views are at any moment in the ascendancy, and which gives us and our students protection as individuals against official pressures toward conformity and orthodoxy. Once we ourselves breach this neutrality by using the university itself and our roles as professors within it to advance political judgments we hold personally, we forfeit the strongest moral link in the chain of our defenses.

In all of the foregoing I have tried to identify what there is in the special calling of the professor and the special role of the university that is imperiled by the strike. But if I have created the expectation, despite my earlier protestations, that I would therefore damn all strikes and those who engage in them or broadly support the imposition of retaliatory university discipline, I must disappoint. For all I feel warranted in concluding is that there is a strong *prima facie* case against the professorial strike, for the reasons I have stated. The infliction of great injuries may be justified by the need to avoid still greater ones and may be excused by pressures and circumstances which challenge the restraint of the most scrupulous. This is as true in the law as it is in the judgments we make in daily life. It is no less true of the strike.

What is also true, however, is that the task of defining those circumstances of justification and excuse does not lend itself to easy or closed formulas. Very much this kind of task has occupied the criminal law for centuries. Over the years specific grounds have been formulated; for example, the law of justification based on self-defense, the defense of another, the prevention of crime, the law of excuse based on duress, superior orders, or necessity. But it is too early in our experience with this new academic challenge to formulate even categories as open and general as these of the criminal law. All one can do, I think, is scrupulously avoid the undiscriminating thinking which denies their existence and try sensitively to attend to the kinds of circumstances which might ground their invocation.

The regularized collective bargaining economic strike represents, for the reasons I tried to suggest, the sharpest subordination of professional ideals. I find it hard to believe that its gain could ever be worth its costs. Yet what should we say of a junior college, for example, which in all respects except its name is run as an extension of the secondary school system with employee-teachers retained to perform allotted tasks of instruction, with decisions hierarchically made in light of goals authoritatively set by those in control, with research and scholarship regarded not even as an appropriate by-product of its main functions? Can we fairly invoke commitments to university ideals when in truth there is no university? We can talk of the public interest in uninterrupted teaching of the young, as we do in the case of schoolteachers. I doubt, however, that we can talk appropriately of professorial and university ideals. In judging strikes of this kind I am not sure we will ever be on safe ground until we recognize the reality that not all that passes as higher education is so in fact. I am suggesting nothing wildly impractical. We already draw a distinction between the schoolteacher and the university professor in these matters. I am only saying that with the increasing proliferation of institutions called colleges and universities that line will have to be drawn out of regard for real functional distinctions instead of labels.

And even in the case of genuine institutions of higher education, the regularized use of strikes in a collective bargaining context must, I think, be distinguished from an *ad hoc* occasion in which a faculty, oppressed beyond endurance by low salaries and burdensome teaching loads, is reduced to striking as a last-ditch effort in self-defense and survival. Even more distinguishable would be a strike to enforce a claim neutrally and judiciously supported, as, for example, by an arbitration award. Moreover, a host of other considerations of time, place, and manner affect the judgment. Is the strike in breach of a contract or is it a refusal to accept a contract? Is it in mid-term or at its commencement? Is it an open refusal to meet classes or a disguised technique of educational sabotage?

So far as the academic interest strike is concerned, justification, or at least excuse, might more readily be found in the degree of academic iniquity to which the university had fallen, the obduracy of the administration to appeals to common commitment and reason, the crisis character of the situation, the absence of effective alternatives, and the like. With all the evils of even altruistically directed strikes, such incidents as that at Catholic University, where the faculty joined the students in a successful boycott protest over an apparently flagrant breach of academic freedom, are sober reminders of the peril of black and white judgments. The central impasse in these situations is like that occasioned by civil disobedience. The risk of damage in bypassing the established mechanisms of reasoned accommodation is great. And one may be wrong, or ill-informed, or carried away, or acting out of all proportion. But just as it has been held that a lawyer may conscientiously disobey some laws without necessarily disqualifying himself for unprofessional conduct,[21] so may a professor sometimes similarly depart from the norms of academic propriety. And the departure from these norms may be less substantial in some cases than in others, as, for example, in a case where the departure from academic freedom had previously been authenticated by a disinterested agency.

Lastly, the political strike. There are political issues and there are political issues. I don't suppose one could have anything but the strongest sympathy for professors under a Nazi-like regime who resorted to whatever pressure they had at their disposal, including use of the university and their professorial roles, to combat governmental evils such as genocide. It has been a conviction long held by many responsible people that there comes a point when a governmental policy extends beyond the ambit of political controversy and poses to citizens the choice only to accede to or resist ultimate evils, all other considerations being dwarfed into insignificance. One can insist that there can be no such point in a democratic system, or that those who feel it has been reached are mistaken and acting out of all proportion, but condemnation comes hard when people act on considerations such as these.

I fear I have now given the impression of having turned squarely around and marched right back along the road I had taken earlier. There is at least this to be said for this tactic—it's a sure way to avoid getting lost. But it's also a sure way of not going anywhere

[21] Hallinan v. Committee of Bar Examiners, 65 Cal. 2d 447, 421 P.2d 76 (1966).

and I hope I have not yielded to the temptation. The risk of creating that impression was one I thought worth taking, as I said earlier, in order to develop as clearly as I could what was wrong with professors striking in varied contexts. Nothing in my later words is meant as the slightest retraction of that analysis. For to give reasons for not doing something is not to say that it should never be done, or that it may not be more defensible under some conditions than others. Only when we have taken care to see precisely what is at stake and why may we begin to make judgments of the special circumstances in which it may be worth the cost.

Now so far I have spoken only of the professor. What of the university, represented by the administration and its governing board? How are they to act in the face of one or another of these kinds of strikes? I would hope with the greatest caution and restraint.

Of course defensive measures may have to be taken. If teaching assistants decline to meet their classes, replacements or reallocations of work will have to be explored. If professors strike for prolonged periods of time, others may have to be sought to take their places; and if a striker's position is filled in consequence, when the battle is over it may be reasonable, on the industrial analogy, to relieve the university of an obligation to accept him back. And payment need generally not be made for services not performed.

But offensive measures are another matter. It goes without saying that when discipline is contemplated the entire pattern of academic procedural due process must be accorded whether the grounds be participation in a strike or anything else. This is crucial not only to assure reliable factual judgments, but also to permit full exploration of the variety of circumstances and conditions which, as I tried to say, may substantially affect the merits of the matter. For the same reasons it would be intolerable to act on the premise that striking is automatically sufficient ground for discharge or other discipline. To be sure, the informal constitution of academic freedom, the 1940 AAUP *Statement of Principles on Academic Freedom and Tenure,* speaks of "neglect of duties" as a ground for discipline. But the term contemplates a very different set of problems than those presented by the strike, which was far from the minds of the 1940 draftsmen. Whatever one's final conclusions, it is plain that cutting classes for personal reasons raises different considerations than striking to obtain some concession from the university.

But even with these cautions, discipline is perilous. In the context of a strike administrators and governing boards are interested parties; indeed, they usually are one of the protagonists. They are in no position to bring a measured and objective judgment to the case. Moreover, to yield to the temptation to retaliate in indignation is to aggravate further those centrifugal forces of divisiveness and disruption which the strike itself set in motion. The long-run maintenance of the conditions of effective university life is no less a responsibility of those who exercise administrative authority than it is of those who do not. Further, a university which has been racked by a strike is almost by definition suffering from profound and deep-rooted problems. Discipline and discharge are quick and easy responses which assuage injured pride. But they are not in themselves ever likely to address the underlying sources of discontent for which, in any event, the ad-

ministration or governing board can never acquit itself
of responsibility. On the contrary, they are calculated
to add to them. I am not urging passive inaction. I
am simply saying that instead of impetuously lopping
off heads in righteous indignation the university authorities would do better to look to themselves and
the sources of the breakdown in an effort to reinvigorate the shared professional commitment to the educational enterprise which is all, in the last analysis, that
can hold the place together.

Finally, discipline of professors (and of students
too, by the way) is a vastly overrated and overin-
dulged means of maintaining the effectiveness of university life. It is only one among many of the sanctions
and influences which operate, and probably the least
effective. There are times when it is inescapable, and
I would not argue that the authority to impose it
should be denied. But, like the strike, discipline is
potentially the most damaging of the means of effect-
ing change or preserving what we want, and should,
no less than the strike, carry a heavy burden of proof
that nothing else will do and that the risk must be
taken. Appeals to common commitment by reason and
persuasion, the pressure of opinion, the judgment of
colleagues—these are the informal sanctions which
cement the academic community and which administrators and governing boards, no less than professors,
have a professional obligation to recognize as the
principal modes of accommodation appropriate for a
university as a community of scholars.

The University's External Constituency

Arthur DeBardeleben

In 1894 the Board of Regents of the University of Wisconsin, in response to a demand of the state superintendent of public instruction that Professor Richard T. Ely be dismissed from the faculty because of alleged heretical writings concerning the trade union movement, adopted the following declaration which has been called by many the Magna Charta of academic freedom in America:

We cannot for a moment believe that knowledge has reached its final goal or that the present condition of society is perfect. We must therefore welcome from our teachers such discussions as shall suggest the means and

ARTHUR DeBARDELEBEN. Ph.B. 1940, LL.B. 1947, University of Wisconsin; Member, Board of Regents of the University of Wisconsin, 1959-68; President of the Board, 1964-67; Member, Wisconsin Coordinating Committee for Higher Education (and of Plans and Policies Subcommittee thereof), 1959-67; General practice of law, Park Falls, Wisconsin.

prepare the way by which knowledge may be extended, present evils removed and others prevented. We would be unworthy of the position we hold if we did not believe in progress in all departments of knowledge. In all lines of academic investigation it is of the utmost importance that the investigator should be absolutely free to follow the indications of truth wherever they may lead.

Whatever may be the limitations which trammel inquiry elsewhere, we believe the great State University of Wisconsin should ever encourage that continual and fearless sifting and winnowing by which alone the truth can be found.[1]

Seventy years later, in 1964, the regents reaffirmed this commitment at the time of the conversion of traditional faculty tenure policies into a legal tenure code, unanimously declaring:

In adopting this codification of the rules and regulations of The University of Wisconsin relating to academic tenure, the Regents reaffirm their historic commitment to security of professorial tenure and to the academic freedom it is designed to protect. These rules and regulations are promulgated in the conviction that in serving a free society the scholar must himself be free. Only thus can he seek the truth, develop wisdom, and contribute to society those expressions of the intellect that ennoble mankind. The security of the scholar protects him not only against those who would enslave the mind, but also against anxieties which divert him from his role as scholar and teacher. . . . The Regents take this opportunity to rededicate themselves to maintaining in this University those conditions which are indispensable for the flowering of the human mind.[2]

[1] RECORDS OF THE BOARD OF REGENTS, UNIVERSITY OF WISCONSIN 295 (Vol. D., Sept. 18, 1894); CURTI & CARSTENSEN, I, THE UNIVERSITY OF WISCONSIN 1848-1925, at 525 (1949).
[2] Minutes, Board of Regents, University of Wisconsin, Jan. 10, 1964.

On October 18, 1967, as the result of protests against recruitment interviews by Dow Chemical Company on the Madison campus of the University of Wisconsin, a confrontation occurred between the protesters and the police. Violence ensued and some of the policemen and about seventy-five of the student protesters were injured. The use of police against the students, the fact that a substantial number of students were injured, and the fact that the protest provided a tangible expression of the revulsion of many students and faculty members to the horror of the Vietnam war resulted in calls for suspension of and boycott against the holding of classes. During the succeeding two or three days approximately 150 faculty members and teaching assistants either did not meet or dismissed their classes. There were demands by a number of politicians and newspapers for punishment of or reprisals against the faculty members and teaching assistants involved. At the meeting of the regents held one month later, the following resolution was moved:

That any teaching assistant or faculty member, who on October 18, 19, 20, 21, or 23rd, 1967, without a legitimate excuse did not appear to conduct his or her class, or dismissed his or her class after assembly on the grounds that the students thereof should participate in or support the strike then in progress, shall be deemed guilty of conduct constituting adequate cause for dismissal and shall be removed from his or her teaching assignments, and shall have his or her employment terminated. . . .[3]

The resolution failed on a vote of 5 to 4.

Essential to the maintainance of academic freedom is a system of tenure based upon rules assuring that

[3] Minutes, Board of Regents, University of Wisconsin, Nov. 17, 1967.

once a faculty member has achieved tenure status, he cannot be discharged except for good cause shown, upon reasonable notice, and following a fair hearing. The tenure code which had been adopted in 1964 followed carefully the standards proposed by the American Association of University Professors in providing academic due process to any faculty member whose continued tenure might be questioned, and provided the procedure, within the organization of the faculty, for the handling of complaints. What, then, caused nearly half of the members of the Board of Regents which had unanimously adopted the tenure code to the accompaniment of the stirring statement quoted above to resolve, three years later, to disregard the tenure code, to enforce a completely ex post facto rule, and to deprive the faculty members and teaching assistants involved of even the forms of due process? The answer to this question goes to the heart of the subject I have been asked to discuss with you today. My charge was to "examine the freedom of the university vis-à-vis the external society"; to address myself to the questions: "What freedom is necessary to the university that it may properly perform its function and its role to the external society? How can such freedom be secured?"

Before addressing the questions, permit me to state briefly the definition of the term "academic freedom" as I understand it and as that term is intended by me when used in these remarks.

It is necessary to look first to the mission of the university—the mission of the scholar. The objective of the university—of the scholar—is primarily the seeking and ascertainment of truth. Truth, in this sense, is that which is discoverable by man through

his powers of investigation and the exercise of his ingenuity. Truth, in this sense, does not refer to any doctrine or belief depending for its origin or validity upon any source or theory of divine inspiration or disclosure. Nor does it mean merely "getting at the facts." Truth, in the academic freedom context, is concerned with facts because of their significance, their relationship, within a system of knowledge. Truth thus consists, in short, of the body of conclusions, opinions, and even theories and beliefs which the scholar draws or derives from his observations, investigations, and cogitations. Truth includes the scholar's explanation of the structure and relationship of things and concepts, and has the same meaning whether thought of from the standpoint of the humanist, the social scientist, or the physical or biological scientist.

In pursuing his mission to discover the truth, the scholar, merely by inquiring or investigating, suggests that there are or may be grounds for questioning previously accepted precepts. In the search for truth, the challenge to existing doctrines, conclusions, and beliefs is never-ending so long as there remain data, relationships, or concepts which require explanation.

Thus, my answer to the question as to the freedom necessary to the university to perform properly its function and its role to the external society is that the university, by which I mean the faculty and students, must have complete and unqualified freedom to inquire and investigate, to interpret data, and to arrive at and announce conclusions, in and out of the classroom, without the fear or reality of sanctions or controls of any kind, whether direct or indirect, whether pecuniary or related to status or advancement, whether from within or from without the institution. This is a societal interest which is independent of, although not superior to, the right of the individual scholar as a citizen to the exercise of freedom of inquiry and expression.

As Professor David Fellman has pointed out in his comment on "Academic Freedom in American Law" in the 1961 *Wisconsin Law Review,* most people, at least when they are speaking publicly, would not today subscribe to the argument of William Jennings Bryan in *Scopes v. State* [4] that "the hand that writes the teachers' paycheck is the hand that runs the schools . . . otherwise, a teacher might teach anything!" Nor, I hope, would many agree with the equally blunt statement of the "hired hand" theory as expounded by State Senator Clayton Lusk of New York that "teachers who are paid out of public funds . . . have no right . . . to believe in . . . changes in the state and national government," or the pronouncement of the executive vice-president of Renssalaer Polytechnic Institute, following dismissal of a literary critic from the faculty because of his political views, that "we adhere to an unwritten regulation of long standing that there shall be excluded from our classroom all controversial discussions about politics, religion, and sociology." [5]

Most people do profess to favor academic freedom. But this does not gainsay the fact that there are external influences which have resulted in the erosion of freedom. A wide variety of subjects have caused difficulty.

[4] 154 Tenn. 105, 289 S.W. 363 (1927).
[5] *See* Fellman, *Academic Freedom in American Law,* 1961 WIS. L. REV. 1.

Clearly, the principal objective of a number of attackers of academic freedom during the last three-quarters of a century has been to suppress economic nonconformity. It is no secret that there are scholars who are critical of aspects of the capitalistic system. Attacks on professors whose investigations lead them to question something old in the quest for something new which will be better than the old rarely take the form of direct argument, contention, or exposition on the merits. Rather, the economic groups affected, or which think they might be affected, by a scholar's investigations or teachings attempt to counter the work of the scholar by the use of such bias characterizations as "fellow travelers," "pinks," "reds," "socialists," "un-American," or "anti-Christian." In using these examples of bias words employed by attackers of academic freedom, I do not intend any distinction depending upon whether the attack comes from the right or from the left. But notwithstanding the denunciations by Students for a Democratic Society, and similar groups, of our universities as institutions which must be brought down because they are instruments of the "liberal corporate structure," it must be admitted that in this country at the present time attacks upon academic freedom which are economically oriented are coming mainly from individuals and groups at the extreme right of the political spectrum. The noteworthy thing about the attackers of economic nonconformity in the academic community is that although their number is small they seem able to portray themselves as protectors of "free enterprise," thus appealing to considerable numbers of persons in the business community who, because their interest in

education is solely as a means to a practical end—
the earning of more money than they could earn without it—have never been inspired by the challenge of
acquiring knowledge for its own sake and who are,
therefore, especially impressed by the argument that
the academic social scientist or humanist is "impractical" or "unreliable."

All of us have been disturbed, at one time or another, about attacks made upon our institutions of
higher learning in the name of religion—attacks which
range all the way from characterizing universities as
being "godless," "atheistic," or "anti-religious" to demands that "departments of religion" be established
and that professors be appointed who will "Christian-
ize" the students. Quite often those who attack academic freedom in the name of religion are also active
in attacks upon our scholars in the name of economic
nonconformity. Professor Robert M. MacIver has
pointed out that "it seems to be as easy for certain
minds to identify the divine law with their economic
predilections as with their religious tenets." [6]

There is another side of the coin with respect to
the relationship between religion and academic freedom. Cases continue to arise when a teacher's moral
or religious convictions lead him to refuse to comply
with some law or regulation or to conform with some
customary standard or to support some cause which
would involve violation of his creed. A conscientious
objector may refuse to obey a draft law or may arouse
even more resentment by taking a strong, public anti-
war position. Conscientious objectors have been dismissed from their academic positions, and I note from

[6] MacIver, Academic Freedom in Our Time (1955).

the public prints that there is, while I am speaking to you, a move afoot in Illinois, at the behest of State Superintendent Ray Page, to forbid students entrance or continuation at the state university because of their views on that subject.[7] One of the members of the board of regents upon which I serve recently inquired, at a board meeting, what qualifications a law professor has to express an opinion on the Vietnam war. We hear increasing demands from Washington and elsewhere to still criticism of our government's military policy, typified by the recent statement of General Westmoreland that "the time has come for debating to end. . . ." It is difficult to conceive a situation showing a greater negation of intellectual freedom than where a faculty member is dismissed, or a student denied admission or expelled, or where either would be obliged to divert his attentions to concern with the possibility of dismissal or other reprisal, because his opinion as to what is good for the country and for humanity, at a given time, differs from that of the military establishment.

Another source of attack upon academic freedom comes from those who, although they would concede that the scholar should not be fettered by economic or religious dogma and, indeed, cannot be constitutionally so fettered, nevertheless believe there is (or should be) an establishment of morality, a "conventional wisdom" governing social relations, which may not be questioned by the scholar, either as investigator, teacher, or citizen. The most troublesome problems concern sex relationships, for example, birth

[7] Superintendent Page's resolution to this effect was subsequently withdrawn. [Ed.]

control or premarital and extramarital sexual conduct. The records are replete with examples of scholars who have been dismissed on charges ranging from membership in the American Sunbathers Association, in the case of a professor of physics at a Tennessee college, to the case of Bertrand Russell, whose removal as professor of philosophy at the College of the City of New York in 1940 was prompted by charges that his books promoted "immoral and salacious doctrines."

Attacks on academic freedom in the name of protection of the mores of sexual conduct are doubly outrageous because in addition to involving an attempt to destroy freedom of inquiry (common to any attack on academic freedom), they involve, in many instances, an utter disregard on the part of the attackers of the gulf which exists between the so-called mores sought to be protected and the actual prevailing social practice. The dismissal, about one year before the expiration of his appointment, of an assistant professor at the University of Illinois because of certain comments which he had made relating to sexual conduct was characterized by Committee A of the American Association of University Professors as creating "substantial concern over the question whether the University [involved] actually will permit untrammeled discussion of highly controversial issues, or whether freedom to express unpopular views will be seriously qualified by the test of 'encouragement' and 'academic responsibility.' " [8] In announcing the reasons for the dismissal of the assistant professor, the institutional president fell back on the old clichés. He stated: "I

[8] *Academic Freedom and Tenure: The University of Illinois,* 49 A.A.U.P. BULL. 25 (1963).

consider [the faculty member's] letter [to a student newspaper] *a grave breach of academic responsibility.* The views expressed are *offensive and repugnant, contrary to commonly accepted standards of morality,* and their public espousal may be interpreted as *encouragement of immoral behavior.* It is clear that . . . [his] conduct *has been prejudicial to the best interests of the University."* [9]

This case is illustrative of the form which attacks on academic freedom may be expected to take in the future, whether these attacks originate from distaste for a professor's views on so-called moral subjects or his views on social, economic, or political subjects. For example, in the June 1963 issue of *American Governing Board Reports,* published by the Association of Governing Boards of State Universities and Allied Institutions, a synopsis of remarks made at a panel discussion of regent responsibilities shows one regent advocating the fostering of an "academic climate which guarantees freedom of *responsible* thinking and research." Another trustee, who said that "it is fatal to select or promote only those faculty members who conform to an acceptable political, social or religious code," saw no inconsistency in declaring that trustees and regents have the duty of *"initiating* dismissal proceedings for a faculty member who may be found to be a member of the communist party."

I have read to you the reasons given by the institutional president for the dismissal of an assistant professor because of the content of a letter on sex mores written to a student newspaper. What did the Board of Trustees have to say on the subject? The board found, among other things, that the assistant profes-

[9] *Id.* at 28 (emphasis added).

sor's letter "was not a *reasoned* statement, marshaling evidence in support of views held by him," and that "the language of that letter was not in keeping with those *standards of temperateness, dignity, and respect for the opinions of others* which should characterize public expression by members of the faculty of the University." [10] The board asserted "that any *responsible* expression of views by the members of the faculty, even though unpopular and even, *possibly,* untenable, is in order," and that it did not condemn the assistant professor's actions "merely because he expressed . . . views contrary to commonly accepted beliefs and standards." Its condemnation was "because of the manner in which he expressed those views in his letter," which the board did "not consider . . . a *'responsible' and proper expression* of the views stated." [11] The Ad Hoc Committee of the American Association of University Professors considered the board's reliance upon irresponsibility and stated: "The concept of 'irresponsibility' is exceedingly vague. Any one of us can easily call to mind statements by our colleagues which might be termed by some as unrestrained, undignified, or lacking respect for the opinion of others. Any serious application of the standard would tend to eliminate or discourage any colorful or forceful utterance. More likely . . . the standard would be reserved as a sanction only for expression of unorthodox opinion." [12] And addressing itself to the letter which precipitated the dismissal, the Ad Hoc Committee observed: "It seems clear to us that, had the letter dealt with any subject other than sex mores, religion, or some other acutely sensitive area, its lan-

[10] *Id.* at 30 (emphasis added).
[11] *Id.* at 31 (emphasis added).
[12] *Id.* at 37.

guage and tone would have passed unnoticed. We do not believe that a faculty member writing on these subjects should be held to higher standards of responsibility than one writing on less controversial topics." [13]

In a free and open society, no value can command higher priority than the right of citizens to freedom of expression. It is indispensable to such a society that the scholar, professionally and as a citizen, be free in an absolute sense from the cares, worries, and distractions that would be imposed by any qualification of this freedom. Professor Warren Taylor properly pointed out in his separate dissent on the case of the assistant professor: "To fire a teacher for his utterances the administrator cannot rely on such an ambiguous test as that of 'academic responsibility.' The opinions of a teacher as citizen are not enough to justify termination. The administrator will have to establish proof that beyond the utterance lies unfitness to teach: professional incompetence, dereliction of duty." [14]

This brief review of the sources of danger to academic freedom must include mention of the influence of political controls and governmental activity. The iniquitous loyalty oaths and disclaimer affidavits required by certain federal enactments and by statutes which have been adopted by a few states—including the obnoxious Clabaugh Act, to which the faculty of this institution is still subjected—illustrate political influence in its most obvious and repugnant forms.[15] Also of great danger is the fact that the growth of

---

[13] *Id.* at 39.
[14] *Id.* at 43.
[15] The Clabaugh Act has since been declared unconstitutional in a federal court. [Ed.]

state appropriations for higher education has resulted in the imposition of hitherto unknown administrative controls upon our colleges and universities. Federal government-sponsored research now determines the subject matter and direction of a major part of the research and scholarly inquiry going on in our universities. The allocation of federal research money has, until very recent years, starved the social studies and humanities in favor of the natural sciences. The high degree of specialization in government-sponsored research has created divisions within the natural sciences which threaten to make the cultural gap which has existed between the humanists and the scientists, physical and social, seem paltry by comparison. It is imperative that the appropriation and acceptance of federal support be conditioned in such a manner as not to deflect scholars from productive work of a basic, theoretical nature in favor of research which offers the promise of practical results and benefits over the short term. It cannot be considered other than an infringement upon academic freedom when a scholar can only get support for research likely to lead to fairly immediate practical results or when the ebb and flow of support for research and scholarly investigation depend upon the current fashion in weaponry, space technology, or the existence or absence of crises in foreign relations or military policy.

If the universities are to pursue their mission with effect, scholars in each discipline must have opportunities for research and scholarly inquiry about equal to the opportunities of scholars in each other discipline. None of this means that research which may result in practical benefits should lack encouragement and support. All of our land-grant universities are justly proud of their outstanding scholars whose investigations and discoveries have made possible many great practical benefits to mankind. We should be equally proud of those whose scholarly inquiries have advanced knowledge in areas having no immediate apparent practical consequences. The encouragement of advancement of basic knowledge should never be dominated by considerations of practicality, popular whim, or current crisis. Freedom in research and scholarly inquiry demands the provision of support, unencumbered by restrictions of any kind, sufficient to permit all faculty members having research competence and inclination to pursue the lines of scholarly inquiry which *they* decide are worthy of investigation.

Now, how can the freedom of the university be secured?

The governing body, whether denominated regents or trustees, the university administration, and the faculty each has an important role in the preservation of academic freedom against challenges from external forces and influences. In addition there has been a growing insistence by the courts, during recent years, that principles of "academic due process" be applied in cases involving the possible discipline or dismissal of a faculty member. Although such cases remain few in number, they do show an increasing realization of the societal interest in preventing abridgements of academic freedom, and a possible resort, in extreme cases, to legal institutions.[16]

But I would like to concentrate upon the roles which should be played by the regents or trustees, the

---

[16] A wide-ranging discussion of developments in the law affecting academic freedom appears in 81 HARVARD L. REV. 1045 (1968). [Ed.]

administration, and the faculty in meeting external threats.

The governing board of a university has a primary duty, in the exercise of its policy-making function, to assure the codification and observance of rules of tenure which guarantee to persons having tenure status the freedom of inquiry, investigation, and expression which I have previously mentioned. A governing board should consult with representatives of the faculties of the institution whenever the necessity for the selection of a new president exists. A governing board should not appoint to the office of president of a university any person who does not have a general consensus of approval of the faculty. In making appointments to academic positions or in deciding upon promotions or transfers, a governing board should act on the advice of the president who, in turn, should have secured the advice of the faculty as a whole or of an appropriate faculty committee. And, in recommending any dismissal from a tenure position, a president should have the concurrence of the faculty.

However, these are but elemental requirements for the maintenance of academic freedom. In addition, a governing board has the responsibility of safeguarding and fostering an environment and an atmosphere unqualifiedly conducive to the free and untrammeled search for truth. It is the duty of a governing board to resist the pressures, clamors, and demands of ideological groups and other special interests—all who would compromise the goals of scholarship—whether alumni, politicians, private donors, the press, or segments of the public. A governing board should protect the faculty and the students against all outside pressures which would divert them from scholarly pursuits.

A president of a university protects and implements academic freedom by interpreting to the public the values and goals of higher education and the primary importance of freedom of inquiry and expression. A university president protects and implements academic freedom by normally following faculty recommendations concerning appointments and promotions, so long as they are within budgetary allotments, and by encouraging full consultation in the case of differences of opinion. Such a president, if he believes that a whole school or department within his institution fails to maintain adequate standards and falls behind the advance of scholarship in its field, will obtain the advice and assistance of other educators in connection with and before making or recommending changes.

When we think of what the faculty can do to protect and implement academic freedom, we are thinking of what the university itself should do, because the faculty is the on-going university. The greatness of a university is directly attributable to the ability and attainments, the dedication, and the inspirational qualities of its faculty. This is not to say that our great universities could exist without the tax dollars and other monies which support and sustain them or that they could continue without the physical facilities which have been provided, or that present and past administrators have not furnished inspired and effective leadership or have not left their permanent marks upon the progress of the institutions; but none of these things would have been of any avail had it not been for the faculties of the institutions.

When we ask, therefore, what the faculty should do to protect and implement academic freedom against threats of external encroachments, the question may be answered simply and briefly. The faculty must exercise, and insist upon its right and duty to exercise, academic freedom without any qualification whatever. When an academic freedom question or issue is presented, it should be met head on and forthrightly. No quarter, accommodation, or compromise can be given or made to or with the opponents of freedom of inquiry and expression. There have been examples in the academic history of some of our leading institutions where attempts at accommodation, avoidance, or compromise were made. Let us look at some.

At the outset I quoted from an 1894 report of the Board of Regents of the University of Wisconsin. The concluding sentence from that quotation has been cast in bronze and fastened to the doorpost at the main entrance to Bascom Hall, the central building on the Madison campus of the University of Wisconsin: "Whatever may be the limitations which trammel inquiry elsewhere, we believe the great State University of Wisconsin should ever encourage that continual and fearless sifting and winnowing by which alone the truth can be found." The words were drafted by President Charles Kendall Adams at the suggestion of Law Professor John M. Olin and were adopted, initially, by a regent committee consisting of a small-town lawyer, a doctor, and a banker. The statement of principles is one which, in the words of James F. A. Pyre, "no subsequent government has had the hardihood to retract." [17]

It does not take away from the importance of the statement to recognize that it was not responsive to the inquiry before the regent committee. Professor Ely had been charged by the state superintendent of

[17] PYRE, WISCONSIN 292 (1920).

public instruction and tried by a committee of the Board of Regents for believing in "strikes and boycotts, justifying and encouraging the one while practicing the other." He was alleged to have threatened to boycott a local firm whose workers were on strike; to have stated that a union man, no matter how dirty and dissipated, was always to be employed in preference to a nonunion man, no matter how industrious and trustworthy; and to have entertained and counseled with a union delegate in his home. It was charged that Ely's books contained the same principles, that they provided a "justification of attack upon life and property," and were "utopian, impracticable or pernicious." Unfortunately, Professor Ely denied the charges rather than, in effect, demurring to them. Although Professor Ely had declared privately that academic freedom was the vital issue, he did not mention this in his answer to the charges. In fact, Professor Ely stated publicly that if the charges were true, they would "unquestionably unfit me to occupy a responsible position as an instructor of youth in a great university."

Professor Ely had valuable allies throughout the academic world, at Wisconsin and elsewhere. But it seems clear that except for the antipathy which the rest of the members of the board felt toward the state superintendent (an ex-officio regent), except for the warm support and helpful guidance of President Charles Kendall Adams, and except for the sagacious suggestion of Law Professor Olin, the University of Wisconsin's Magna Charta of academic freedom would have had to wait for another occasion. Professor Edward W. Bemis, who ran afoul of the authorities at the University of Chicago at about the same time on similar grounds, perceived that although Ely had won the case, he had sacrificed the important principle. When he wrote to congratulate Ely, he stated: "That was a glorious victory for you. I was sorry only that you seemed to show a vigor of denial as to entertaining a walking delegate or counseling strikers as if either were wrong, instead of under certain circumstances a *duty*." [18]

The California loyalty oath debacle of the 1950's is also instructive. The case points up emphatically the danger of any concession to or appeasement of enemies of academic freedom. It shows that concessions are not only wrong in principle but disastrous in application. Under the threats of the infamous Tenney Committee, the president of the University of California drafted and submitted to the Board of Regents a loyalty oath which was to be required of every faculty member. It was the hope of the president and his advisors that the taking of this step would stave off the more drastic assaults on academic freedom which were being threatened by the Tenney Committee. But the result of the adoption of a requirement for the loyalty oath—afterwards rescinded when the balance of power on the Board of Regents was changed by virtue of appointments made by former Governor Earl Warren—was to invite greater excesses by the Tenney Committee in its assaults on academic freedom and civil liberties. One may sympathize with the harassment which was undergone by the officials of the California institutions, but it is impossible to believe that had they stood up against the onslaught, they could not have turned it back.

[18] HOFSTADTER & METZGER, THE DEVELOPMENT OF ACADEMIC FREEDOM IN THE UNITED STATES 434 (1955).

Strong faculty resistance has been successful. In 1910, the Board of Regents of the University of Wisconsin undertook to make promotions and adjustments of salaries without the recommendations of the appropriate departments or the president, failed to make promotions recommended by the departments and the president, and consulted directly with members of the faculty concerning their own work and that of other departments, thereby showing "a disposition to take the initiative in strictly educational matters, even extending to the point where one regent attended and in a critical way took part in a doctoral examination." Upon strong representations being made by the faculty, the regents backed off and concurred in a statement to the effect that they had "no intention of interfering with the customary methods of educational administration by the faculty . . . they will continue to allow the faculty the initiative in formulating educational policy . . . they desire appointments to be made through the regular channels as developed in the custom of the University." [19]

The opposition to the Illinois Broyles Commission investigation of the University of Chicago and Roosevelt University by the administrations and faculties of those two institutions illustrates, again, the effect of a strong faculty position in support of academic freedom. The recommendations of the Broyles Commission were for legislation to reject any teachers who were members of any "communist front" organization on the Attorney General's list, the dismissal of any student from any tax-supported institution who stated that he was a communist, the ban of sale of any communist literature within colleges and universities, the

[19] CURTI & CARSTENSEN, *supra* note 1, II, at 60-62.

scrutiny of textbooks, and the like. Eight of the proposed measures failed to pass the Illinois legislature
and the ninth was vetoed by Governor Stevenson.

An important part of the responsibility of the faculty to oppose, without equivocation, compromise, or
accommodation, every assault upon or threat to academic freedom is the duty of faculty members to sustain each other. In this day of increased specialization
and multi-campus universities, it may be difficult for
a faculty representing a myriad of disciplines to see
how violations of academic freedom that affect colleagues in departments remote from their own should
be matters of great concern. Although each scholar
has his own field and his own viewpoint, the university
which brings all scholars together has no particular
field and no particular viewpoint save the dedication
to freedom in all of its aspects. The institution which
brings all scholars together is concerned with the
whole body of truth; it has one goal, the discovery
and dissemination of truth. It should make a single
demand upon its members, but it should make that
demand insistently and unceasingly—the demand for
unremitting devotion to the cause of advancement of
knowledge.

The courts have begun, in recent years, to lend
support to the principles of academic freedom and
tenure and have rejected earlier cases holding that
there could be no judicial review at all in situations
involving the dismissal of professors. In addition to
insistence upon the procedural forms of academic due
process, the courts have indicated a willingness to review certain substantive issues of academic freedom,
for example, loyalty oaths and, presently being challenged, that infamous affront to freedom represented

by the speaker ban. But the only sure bulwark in defense of the freedom of the university against attempted impingements upon academic freedom on the part of external society must come from the continuing and insistent demands of the governing boards and faculties of the institutions and their patient and unremitting exposition of the indispensable values of free universities to an open, progressive, and dynamic democratic society.

The New Student and His Role in American Colleges

Edward J. Bloustein

In his study of life in the France of Louis XIV, entitled *The Splendid Century,* W. H. Lewis describes with a fine irony the growing revolutionary sentiment of the French peasantry:

And then there was a nasty spirit abroad in the village; the people were getting impudent, slacker about paying their feudal dues, and sulking about the performance of Manorial Corvées. In some districts peasants have begun "to stare proudly and insolently" at their lord, and are putting their hands in their pockets instead of saluting him. . . . A noble has been executed for squeezing his peasants a little too hard; it is becoming quite common

EWARD J. BLOUSTEIN. B.A. 1948, New York University; B.Phil. 1950, Wadham College, Oxford University; Ph.D. 1954, LL.B. 1959, Corenll University; Professor of Law, New York University Law School, 1961-65; President, Bennington College, 1965 to date.

for peasants to go to law with their seigneur. Things have come to a pretty pass in France.

And so too have things come to a pretty pass in American higher education! There is a nasty spirit abroad on the college campus; students are growing impudent; sulking and unwilling simply to attend classes and take notes, they are protesting, striking, sitting in, demanding a voice in the governance of their colleges, staring proudly and insolently at college presidents and professors alike.

American colleges and universities are undergoing a constitutional crisis. Students are seeking a new role in academic life. The purpose of this paper is to inquire into the causes and the nature of student assertion of a right to share in the management of the American college and university.

The classical American college, against which the ire of students is directed, was a place of serene social relationships and scholarly detachment. Trustees, president, faculty, and students each had a well-established place in a well-ordered hierarchy. Self-appointed trustees, acting as representatives of the general public or some specialized religious community, determined the goals of the college and hired a president to implement these chosen goals. The president then hired a faculty to teach what he believed had to be taught and he admitted students to the college to learn what he believed had to be learned.

President, faculty, and students lived together in the bucolic isolation of their campus, each fulfilling a pre-established role in a universe ordered by the trustees' vision. Students were responsible to the faculty for fulfilling their academic duties and to the president and his staff for living the life of gentlemen. Faculty were responsible to the president for fulfilling their teaching duties and comporting themselves as scholars and men of good breeding. And, finally, the president was responsible to the trustees for maintaining the internal harmony of the system and directing it toward its ordained ends.

The congruity and consistency of this classical academic community was assured as much by its system of educational values as it was by its hierarchical structure. The intention and unifying purpose of the institution was to transmit a received system of learning and culture. The knowledge to be transmitted was considered to be relatively fixed and it was systematically arranged into convenient and appropriate subject matter areas, one relating to another in the same harmonious order which was found in nature. The social tradition which was to be inculcated was likewise characterized by its fixity and its conformity to well-established social expectations.

The student's role in this classical college is simple to describe. A college education was available to and important for a relatively small segment of the population: learning the liberal arts was considered a costly luxury. The student was thus doubly privileged —privileged to be among those chosen to attend college at all, and privileged to be among those who could afford to do so. And, of course, one privilege reinforced the other.

The privileged student did not go to college, he was sent. His relationship to the college was a contractual one, and the contract concerned was what lawyers term a third-party beneficiary contract. Under such a contractual scheme, one party obliges himself to another to have that other party provide a benefit in goods or services to some third party. In this instance, parents paid tuition to the college in consideration of the college providing a benefit for their child in the way of educating him.

Since they carried somewhat the sense of a charitable relationship, the early history of such third-party beneficiary contracts—the history relevant for our purposes in this paper—left no room to the beneficiary, the object of charity, to have a voice over any incidents of the contract. Appropriate to this tradition of the law of contracts as well as to his status as a privileged person, the student was in no position to require anything of his college or to enforce obligations against it; he simply accepted the education given to him.

Still another factor explains the passivity and docility of the traditional student. He was young in an age in which youth was not in fashion and at a time when parents took an assertive and autocratic stance toward their children. It is, I know, now difficult for us to evoke the sense of that day when parents were true "parents" and when being young, although not a disease, was still considered an incapacity. There can be no legitimate doubt, however, that this facet of the cultural climate underlay and reinforced the traditional student's sense of his servile, childlike status in his relationship to his college.

It is not difficult to understand how, under these circumstances, the doctrine of *in loco parentis* grew, flourished, and came to embody the college's conception of its relation to its students. Dealing with young people in a day when it still rang true to say "children are to be seen, but not heard," educating them under a third-party beneficiary contract enforcible only by a parent, and recognizing them as among a class privileged to be in college at all, it seemed natural, appropriate, and just to look on the college as the student's substitute parent. The parent having given over his child to the college authorities for the purpose of his education, these authorities came to act in lieu of parents, empowered by law, custom, and usage to direct and control student conduct to the same extent that a parent could.

The fitting image is of the college president as the academic father and students as the dutiful children of learning: wise in his choice of what the young ones were to study; dedicated and enlightened in his mission as moral guardian over them; stern but just as their disciplinarian. and yet a man sufficiently attached to life's joy to provide his young with wholesome and healthy—necessarily nonsexual—outlets for fun and games.

This is the picture of the "classical" college president and his academic wards. Students either had to fit into this picture or else they left the sacred academic precincts. They had no other choice than, in the words of the Illinois Supreme Court written in that dark era, to "yield obedience to those who, for the time being, are their master."

There are those, I am certain, who look back longingly to the classical American college in which trustees, president, faculty, and students, each knowing their own place, revolved about the central sun of certain knowledge in orbital harmony. My own evocation of the past of our colleges serves an entirely different need, however. For one thing, I have no regret over the old order having passed; what praise it merits for its stability and fixity of purpose is surely over-balanced by its intellectual anemia, its myopic vision of its social function, and its insufferable class bias. For another thing, however, for good or for ill, the winds of change have blown, and we must look to what is past not to savor it or forswear it but to learn what we can from it.

To be sure, the view which I have presented of what I have called the classical American college is incomplete and wanting; it is a kind of historical caricature. Like other caricatures, however, it is intended to grasp and emphasize what is essential, even if it does so at the expense of some distortion. What marked the classical college was a hierarchical structure of authority, a fixed and ordered system of certain knowledge, a rigidly defined and severely limited set of educational functions, and a completely paternalistic relationship between student and college. The breakdown of the classical college system and the emergence of the new student may be traced, among other causes, to weaknesses in each of these characteristic elements of it.

This is not the place, of course, to discuss all of the causes of the dissolution of the classical system and the emergence of modern colleges and universities. It is enough for my purposes here to examine three of the chief engines of change: expansion in and transformation of the character of the body of knowledge that the university is called upon to nurture and transmit, the development of the social function that education is called upon to perform, and the emergence of the new student. Each of these changes has profoundly affected the organizational structure of the academic community and the student's role in it.

Contemporary knowledge is more a congeries of discrete and specialized truths than a unified system, and the congeries keeps growing and growing in size and complexity. Moreover, the extent of what we know is such that few men can profess anything but a relatively narrow segment of the body of our knowledge. Still further, we may say that, with the exception of mathematics and the subject areas it touches, deductive certainty has played a more and more insignificant role as a style of thought; the tentative empirical hypothesis, shifting and changing explanations of observable facts, have come to typify our way of thinking. The final characteristic of contemporary knowledge which is significant in this context is that it has become increasingly useful to and important for us. Knowledge is a necessity of life in the intricate social, political, and economic structure of the contemporary world.

Each of these characteristics of the corpus of our knowledge has had a marked effect on the college community. No longer can a board of trustees and a college president pretend to even a bare acquaintance with, no less a mastery over, the range of subjects the college teaches. Their attempts to manage and oversee what is taught necessarily reflect this fact. Under the circumstances, the faculty must look to their peers, within and without the college, for guidance and supervision in the performance of their teaching functions. And this, of course, represents a radical breach in the classical scheme of the organization of the college. Faculties can no longer be responsible, in any realistic sense, to presidents and lay boards for what they teach and how they teach it.

Still another consequence of the changed character

of contemporary knowledge is that the curriculum has lost both its unity and what I might call its preemptive character. The complexity, diversity, and specialization of contemporary thought make it impossible to fix upon any single set or even any small number of sets of subjects of study which can be considered basic or fundamental to higher education. Under these circumstances, method and the process of inquiry are bound to take on more importance than subject matter competence. And the varied interests, skills, capacities, and inclinations of students come to be a more meaningful determinant of what they should study than any predetermined and fixed order of universally prescribed courses.

The impact of this on the organization of the college is once again to impair the classical hierarchy of dominance and control. Those who would prescribe a course of study, whether boards, presidents, or faculty, are increasingly at a loss to say what is to be prescribed. The very diversity and specialization of what we teach in the contemporary college makes it impossible to lay down with any assurance what anyone should learn.

This same influence on attempts to prescribe a settled curriculum arises from the empirical and non-deductive character of our knowledge. Instead of a single corpus of learning strictly ordered by the canons of logic and carrying the weight of an established tradition, we find discrete and shifting sets or families of theories, only loosely bound together and constantly shifting, as observation and new theoretical insight restructure entire fields of science. Who shall say, who can say, what is settled and enduring, what is fundamental to the educational process, in the face of this? Whoever has insight into this facet of the logic, the history, and the sociology of knowledge must in modesty confess that attempts at prescribing a fixed and universal curricular organon are doomed to failure.

I urge, then, that the constitutional structure of the classical college has been impaired in two important respects by the development of our system of knowledge. The claim on the part of lay boards and presidents to exercise exclusive control over what is taught and how it is taught in the college has given way simply on account of obvious, though of course far from blameworthy, incompetence. And the boards' and presidents'—even the faculties'—claim to exercise exclusive control over what must be learned has given way because of the specialization, diversity, and shifting empirical character of what is taught.

Although I shall develop this thought as I proceed, I might say in a preliminary fashion, at this point, that the constitutional role of students has been affected by each of these two revisions in the structure of the college community. Once the college faculty has successfully challenged the legitimacy of the board's and the president's exclusive role in determining educational policy, the whole classical structure of authority is threatened and students can begin to ask why boards and presidents should solely determine anything else. This same skeptical and corrosive doubt flows from the increasing weakness evidenced in authoritative attempts to prescribe a curriculum.

The final facet of the development of our system of knowledge which has affected the student's role in his college is directly related to the second major influence mentioned previously as having undermined the classical college. What we teach in colleges has come to have greater and greater utility for our society and this, in turn, has caused our society to look on the college in an entirely new light. Whereas formerly the function that the college performed was limited and of interest to a relatively small segment of the community, the contemporary college and university fulfill a multitude of social tasks which are of considerable importance to the society as a whole.

The traditional college prepared a privileged minority to take roles in society as members of a governing elite and as practitioners of a small number of the genteel professions; the research and scholarship carried out in it bore the mark of origin in the ivory towers of academia. The burgeoning of knowledge in the physical and social sciences and its usefulness to society at large has now led to the appearance of a whole range of new professions and occupations which engage the interest and capacity of the broadest segments of our population. Moreover, academic research and scholarship now directly service our economy and our political and social life on a vast and unprecedented scale. Educational institutions have become a major and vital national resource rather than a peripheral upper-class luxury.

The transition in the importance of higher education in our national life is shown most graphically by comparison of enrollment figures and by examination of some financial data. The enrollment in colleges and universities in 1869 was 52,000, .1 per cent of the general population and 1.1 per cent of the 18–24-year-olds; by 1910 it had grown to 355,000, .4 per cent of the general population and 2.9 per cent of the 18–24-year-olds; by 1963 it had grown to 4,234,000,

2.2 per cent of the general population and 23.3 per cent of the 18–24-year-olds.

In terms of public funding of education, the figures are no less dramatic. Up until this decade, federal funds expended for higher education were almost negligible. But in 1965 the federal government spent $1.9 billion and in 1966 it spent $2.6 billion directly on higher education. In addition to these funds, the federal government made grants of $3.2 billion in 1965 and $3.6 billion in 1966 to educational institutions for research activities. In these same years, 1965 and 1966, state governments expended $3.9 billion and $4.4 billion respectively for higher education. Combined state and federal expenditures in these two years represented some 58 per cent of the total cost of higher education in America.

It is plain that for good or for ill education has gone public. It is vested with a national interest and increasingly funded out of the public purse. There is every indication that the trend in this direction will increase rather than diminish in the coming years. The consequence of this development is to erode still further the structure of trustee and presidential authority.

Some of the erosion is quite direct, some of it indirect. Most federal funding is advanced for specified educational purposes, rather than general operating costs. In the case of research funds, the money most often goes directly to the academic researcher and the college or university has virtually no control over its expenditure. In the case of other funds, the college can only say yea or nay to a grant for a specific purpose and very frequently, considering the penury of most academic budgets, there is really no choice.

Thus, trustees and presidents have in good measure been forced to abdicate real control over their expenditures to become bookkeepers of public funds.

The indirect effects of the widespread public interest in and support of higher education are even more important for our purposes. Even if federal funding did not limit the trustees' and presidents' available managerial options, it would still vastly diminish their power. Use of public funds in higher education calls for a degree and kind of public accountability, of responsibility to the public at large, which goes far beyond the vague and self-enforced sense which the traditional trustee and president had of representing the community interest. This change is reinforced by the fact that faculty and students alike—the low men on the traditional totem pole of academic power—are part of that public to which the trustee is accountable. Thus, the nature and extent of the trustees' and presidents' authority must necessarily be changed and diminished when they begin to expend and control funds which they do not themselves donate or generate.

Another aspect of the new public interest in education is that it gives college faculty a new sense of their social status, a sense which is at variance with their traditional subservient role in the collegiate hierarchy. They are no longer creatures of a benign alma mater's largesse. They are valued social operatives, sought after to fulfill important tasks in the economy and government and equally sought after by other academic institutions suffering from a faculty shortage caused by swollen enrollments.

No longer will a student look with awe and wonder at the college president and believe that the president controls the destiny of the great scholars with whom students study. Prestigious faculty now make and break colleges, buy and sell college presidents, as they say. Both faculty and students are well aware of this dramatic reversal of position and what its consequences are for the college power structure.

Still another facet of what we might call the nationalization of education is that members of the public in unprecedented numbers and coming from social strata and classes never before heard from in the halls of academia are now personally concerned with collegiate and academic affairs. Government officialdom, employers, professionals, workers, and parents of widely varying background all now feel a vital interest in a new-found national resource, and they expect it to meet their needs. No longer is the college the preserve of the few, to be watched over and nurtured by magnanimous and wealthy donors and wistful, teary-eyed alumni. The college is *everyman's* garden to be cared for and intended to suit *everyman's* taste and interest.

The last of the challenges to the classical college tradition is directed at the conception of the college serving *in loco parentis,* directed at the paternalism embodied in the collegiate hierarchy of authority. This challenge arises from a number of causes. In the first place, the very conception of the role and authority of parents has changed slowly over a period of time. Increasingly, parents have come to rely on reason and suggestion rather than status and command as the essential elements of their control over their children. Many parents, practicing the cult of permissiveness, have come to eschew any and all forms of discipline, and even more have come to use discipline sparingly and only as a last resort. Finding one's self, self-expression, and individual development have come to displace parental guidance and social standards of conformity as the molders of character and personality. All of these changes have contributed to the development of a generation of new students who instinctively react against authority, academic or otherwise.

The second cause of the breakdown of the paternalistic pattern of collegiate life is a changed attitude toward the nature of the learning process. The traditional student was a relatively more passive participant in the learning process than is the new student. Memory and deductive forms of reasoning were formerly more important student tools than imagination, observation, and criticism. The new student is asked to learn by coping with his subject of study in the same way his teacher does; he is not asked so much to listen to his teacher as to do what his teacher does. He learns by doing and experiencing rather than remembering and deducing. Learning increasingly becomes a form of apprenticeship rather than a form of tutelage.

This changed conception of the learning process finds its way into the earliest school years and reaches its culmination, or should, in college study. Its impact on the constitutional organization of colleges is profound and in many respects similar to that of the changed character of knowledge systems described above. Just as the increasing complexity and specialization and the decreasing deductive unity and fixity of knowledge have weakened the authority of those who would pretend to prescribe curricula and otherwise control what is taught, so too the same result arises out of the changed conception of the learning process.

To the degree that the student becomes an active and creative element in his own education rather than a passive recipient, he comes to resist and resent those who seek to determine for him what he should learn. The very intellectual independence and critical judgment which are fostered and desired as tools of learning are corrosive of the authority of faculty and academic administration. "It is so because the president and trustees say so" is no more an answer to be respected in fixing on a course of study or style of life on campus than "it is so because Aristotle said so" is an answer to be respected in discussion of a philosophical or aesthetic problem in the classroom.

A third factor which tends to undermine the capacity of the college to act as a substitute parent is the new social attitude toward attending college. The traditional student was sent to college by his parents and felt it a privilege to be there. The new student goes to college because he knows it is necessary for him; his parent and, increasingly, his society pay his way because, under the conditions of modern life, a college education is as much his right as a high school education is.

In these circumstances, the college must begin to regard its role as that of a social agent performing a socially valued function rather than merely that of a private agent of a parent undertaking an educational task the parent pays for. It is not the parent who puts the student into college but the society, and in educating a student the college is not acting in the parent's name but in society's.

Moreover, although the student obviously benefits

from his education, it is regarded as a necessity rather than a privilege by his society, which also derives benefit from it. The new student's attitude, even when a parent pays for his education, reflects the changed status of education as a social necessity rather than a private luxury in modern life. However thankful and appreciative of his education he may be, the student need not feel that anyone is doing him a remarkable favor for which he must be beholden and for which he must pay by adopting a respectful and deferential attitude toward authority.

Gone then is the older notion of a third-party beneficiary contract in favor of the privileged student who retained no right to control its incidents. In its place is a new status relationship in which the college performs a socially prescribed task in a manner over which the society generally, including the student, retains considerable control.

The private contract is now replaced by a public duty. In the transition, the paternalism of the older form of the relationship between student and college has become an anachronism.

The fourth and final cause of the breakdown of collegiate paternalism which I shall examine is the changed character of the student body itself. In the last century we have experienced almost a hundred-fold increase in the size of our collegiate student body, a change, as I have already indicated, from a student body comprised of 1 per cent of the 18–24-year-olds 100 years ago to 23.3 per cent of them today. These new students come from social classes and national and racial backgrounds never before present on college campuses in such numbers. They are bright and mature, alienated from traditional values, and newly aware of their political power. This adds up to a radical change in the character of the collegiate student body and the purport of this change is to strain still further the traditional organization of collegiate authority.

The new student is not older than the traditional student but he has had more experience of life. He comes from homes and family backgrounds which have been less isolated from the economic and social struggle. The very style of family life in which he has been brought up is more open and honest; it has made him more aware of what life is really about. He is a product of a better primary and secondary education. And, finally, he shows the effect of the communications revolution; he is a child of television and the film industry.

The sum of these influences has brought forth a generation of young people which is more sensitive to life in all its dimensions than any generation before it has been. These young people have vicariously experienced the whole range of human emotions and been witness to the whole play of political passions: love and hatred; war, greed, and bloodshed; discrimination, hunger, and deprivation; electioneering and rioting. They have seen it all in ways which were not possible before the advent of the television tube. These new students have received the message from the media and they exhibit its mark in their maturity of bearing and purpose.

The second characteristic of the new student which is important for our purposes is his alienation from traditional values and institutions. To be sure, there have been disaffected students before this time. The difference now is in the extent of the disillusion: it is more widespread and it bites more deeply into the range of life's values than it ever has before.

War, poverty, and racial discrimination all loom as fundamental and insurmountable political outrages. Infidelity, divorce, illegitimacy, bureaucratization, and mass conformity appear as poisonous and ineradicable social diseases. And the individual is thought to be inevitably threatened by increasing isolation, loneliness, and boredom. There is nothing to look forward to except losing one's soul in exchange for the dross of material wealth. The old values have failed and there are no new ones to take their place. All the ideologies, all the utopias—from democratic capitalism to Christian salvation to Marxist socialism—seem to have failed. The only heroes left are those who preach destruction, with no other vision of the social good.

This is indeed a generation of rebels without a cause, a generation of nihilists, a generation despairing of the life we live and set on remaking it, but without a vision of any alternative.

And yet the new student is a very political person. Again, of course, we can acknowledge the fact that student generations before this have played the political game. The difference here, as with this generation's alienation, is a difference of degree. Not small political cells, or ineffectual weekly political discussion groups, but impressively large numbers of activists are dedicated with all their being to the pursuit of their political purposes.

In the struggle over the civil rights issue and over the Vietnam war they found a first taste of political success. No other generation of young people has had such political effect, none has been so heralded by journalists or so courted by politicians. They have quite suddenly achieved a sense of their own authority, a sense of the growing force of their own numbers, a sense of identification with the older European and Latin American tradition of student political power. Most important of all, they have developed a distinctive style of political action and a distinctive form of political tactics.

Thus, although the new student is alienated and lacks the conviction of an ideology, he is outraged by evil and thereby transformed into a political person. Disillusioned with traditional political programmatic goals, he stands and fights on limited particular issues. Disillusioned with traditional party and parliamentary politics, he confronts social wrongs directly, attempting limited and immediate remedies. Disillusioned with adult politicians, he has himself become a politician.

The impact of the three characteristics of the new student which I have described on the structure of collegiate authority has been extraordinary. No generation so bright and mature, so alienated from traditional values, and so political in its bearing could conceivably tolerate the paternalism of the classical collegiate system. The new student's maturity and his politicalization, combined with the influence of the other developments which I previously described, make attempts on the part of trustees and administration to prescribe courses of study authoritatively seem ever more illegitimate. The more mature student, seeking to have his education serve his new values and new political goals, wants and needs more of a voice in what he shall study and what the educational goals and values of the college shall be.

As for parietal rules, these seem ever more absurd. The values and style of life embodied in the campus rules of the "Old Coll" were born of a different time, a time which had not yet seen the unmasking of the sexual hypocrisy of the adult world, a time in which college students were tender and innocent young things who had to be protected from evil.

The new student, coming frequently from a different class and culture than the traditional student, is deeply impressed by the contrast in his values and those embodied in the rules of the traditional college. He is suspicious of the trustees and the college president because they are representatives of a value system and of a time that he is in the act of rejecting. Under the circumstances he sees no good reason to accept the authority of the trustees and college president over the conditions of his social life.

The intransigence of the classical collegiate system in the face of these student claims for new freedom and power has reinforced the strains of the underlying conflict. An unheeding structure of collegiate authority has caused the new student to begin to look upon college life as a replica of the wider world from which he is alienated. Trustees and presidents begin to assume the aspect of authoritarian oppressors, enforcing their own system of values on oppressed and powerless students, robbing them of their dignity and impairing their opportunity to pursue the true academic life. Faculty begin to appear to have sold out and abandoned their calling: instead of serving as prophets of a new and better world, they have been seduced to collaboration with the military-industrial establishment by the lure of lucrative contracts. The curriculum seems empty and unimportant, out of tune with our times, irrelevant to our agonies and needs. The goals and purposes of colleges and universities seem to have been subverted from open-minded criticism of the established social order to authoritarian forms of protection and service of that conservative order. And underneath all these other appearances there is the specter of the university as a bureaucratic machine controlled by irresponsible elites and as petty, inhuman, undemocratic, and unresponsive as the world beyond the ivy-covered walls.

A structure of constitutional authority is a delicate thing. Compounded of force and implicit threats of force, of unquestioning acquiescence, habitual obedience, responsiveness to felt need, and an aura of moral fitness, it can only persist if each of these elements continues to contribute its saving balance. It now seems plain that the traditional hierarchical organization of collegiate power must either deliberately readjust to new realities or be transmuted by the impact of discontent.

Radical changes in the system of knowledge, in the social interest in knowledge, and in the student population have all combined to unhinge the delicate balance of academic authority. Acquiescence in and habitual obedience to the traditional structure have begun to dissolve under the actuality of a new relationship of faculty and students to presidents and trustees. The unresponsiveness of academic authority to the felt needs of students and to the changed conditions of academic life has slowly eroded the sense of that authority's moral fitness to govern. Under the circumstances, no matter how strong the force used or threatened, the college and university can never be the same again.

Student activists as well as apologists and defenders of the traditional order are both mistaken about the character of the constitutional revolution in academia. The activists, whether out of ignorance or assumed tactical necessity, conjure up images of the college more appropriate to 100 years ago than today, and they urge political tactics as mistaken as their image of the college.

As with all revolutions, the seeds of this one were laid over a long period of time and the foundations of the old order have long since been undermined by the growth of new sprouts of faculty and student authority. Trustees and presidents of a number of institutions have long since abandoned in fact, if not in law, any pretensions to absolute power and have been seeking diligently for a new form of order. Thus, what Riesman and Jencks call "the Academic Revolusion" is proceeding apace. The need now is as much to consolidate and give structure to changes which have already taken place as it is to exert the pressure of opinion against enclaves of the old tradition. Deliberation about and thoughtful discussion of the new constitutional order should have as high a priority as strident demands and militant tactics directed against the old constitutional order.

Once it is agreed, as many would now agree, that trustees and presidents can no longer exercise absolute power over the academic world, once it is agreed that faculty and students must play a real and substantial role in academic government, a whole series of profound and complex problems arises. How precisely shall power be distributed among trustees, president, faculty, and students? If the hierarchical structure of power is inappropriate, what should replace it? What is the appropriate sphere of each of the organs of power and how are the relationships between these organs and their various jurisdictions to be arranged?

Many colleges and universities are already deeply involved in addressing themselves to these issues and others like them. Some are doing this quite consciously; others as a facet of unconscious throes of change and transition, while still maintaining the fiction of the traditional structure.

Many a revolution has been lost after it had succeeded because those who favored and fought for change neglected to concern themselves with what was to follow the disappearance of the old order. It would be folly of the gravest character to undo the traditional academic structure only to have it replaced with one less just and more inadequate. One of the most significant dangers we face in this regard is that some of the very tactics used to complete the work of reordering the structure of academic authority promise to prejudice the result unalterably. To be sure, there is still resistance in the academic world to abandoning the old forms of authority. And to be sure, this resistance must be overcome by organized political effort. But if there was ever a political struggle in which violence and illegality were unnecessary and inappropriate, this is one. If there was ever a political struggle in which violence and illegality were calculated to destroy the very fruits of victory which are sought, this is one.

The fact is that, for the reasons I have set forth at length, the traditional forms of power are already fast crumbling. The change is already in the works and its pace is quickening. Allies in the form of sympathetic trustees, presidents, and faculty are at hand. Tactics of violence are antithetical to deliberation, the very essence of the academic life. Under the circumstances, students with romantic, stereotyped, and anachronistic conceptions of revolution, students whose need to undertake violent political action is a function more of personal and emotional than of political necessity, should exercise restraint over their revolutionary fantasies. The violence they unleash may, on occasion, produce a temporary aura of success, but it threatens the long-range prospect for building the college and university we desire. As Paul Goodman put it in a slightly different context: "Out of the shambles can only come the same bad world."

Defenders of the old order also suffer under a number of illusions. The first and most important of these is that the whole "fuss," "the so-called revolt," is the work of a few ill-mannered, loud-mouthed radicals. The truth of the matter is, however, that revolutions call forth leaders; leaders never call forth revolutions. Leaders can never create social upheaval; they can only ride its crest. As I have shown in the main body of this paper, the erosion of the traditional structure of academic authority which we are presently witnessing flows from developments in the character of knowledge, in the social uses to which knowledge is put, and in the psychology of our students. It is these underlying social facts which are responsible for transforming the academic world, rather than any group of student leaders. Even if all our student activists were to disappear miraculously, the fundamental maladjustment in the organization of collegiate power would remain.

Too many of our academic leaders have mistaken

the true nature of the student revolt. They are confused because at different times it appears to be ad-
dressed to one or another of different relatively insignificant or, even when not insignificant, relatively
isolated facets of college life. First it is free speech
on campus, then it is visitation hours in student rooms,
then admissions and scholarships for Negro students,
then recruitment of students by war industries, then
the building of a gymnasium in an urban slum, then
the contract relationship between the university and
a defense research corporation. The connection between these seemingly isolated forays is that they all
represent a testing of the academic decision process,
they all go to challenge the legitimacy of the constitutional apparatus of the college or university.

These incidents are not only related to each other,
they are also related to the more profound challenges
posed to the structure of the college which I have
discussed above. In other words, the student activists
have chosen to lay the gauntlet down, not only on
issues which have extraordinary immediate political
appeal, but also on issues which go to test the academic hierarchy and thereby reinforce and find rein-
forcement from the underlying causes of imbalance in
the structure of academic authority. A failure to appreciate these relationships promises a failure to be
able to cope successfully with the problems they
present.

A related facet of the misunderstanding of the nature of the student revolt concerns an underestimation
of the amount of support it finds on university campuses and elsewhere. It is significant and symbolic of
this failure generally that just the other day the police,
who had been called to cope with disturbances on

the Columbia University campus and did a poor job
of it, complained that their failure was attributable in
part to the fact that the administration of the college
had grossly underestimated the number of students
who were sitting in in their buildings.

I am certain that the experience at Columbia will
turn out, after we have studied it, to be much like that
at Berkeley in respect of the fact that—as the Berkeley Muscatine Report demonstrates—the activists "succeeded" because they had wide support, not only
among students generally, but among faculty and
among the lay public as well. The reason for this
support at Berkeley, Columbia, and elsewhere is not
only traceable to the appeal of the particular political
issues on which the ruckuses were raised, but also to
the fact that the issues concerned evoked the support
of all those—faculty, students and laymen alike—
who question the underlying structure of collegiate
authority.

The second important illusion under which many
defenders of the traditional college suffer concerns
remedies. There are some "academic statesmen"—
fortunately few in number—who insist that if the students do not appreciate what they have, let them
leave or be "kicked out," and that this will represent
a solution to the contemporary crisis. After all, they
add, students do not attend college under coercion; if
they do not choose to conform let them leave.

I believe that some students should indeed be disci-
plined, and more generally that the order of the college community should be maintained during this
difficult transition period. There are indeed a number
of students who, because of political naiveté, political
romanticism, or plain malevolence, are bent on de-

stroying what most needs to be saved and rebuilt. And there are a greater number of other students who find in the contemporary situation of stress a rationalization for ill-mannered, selfish, and boorish disregard of the rights of others. But anyone who supposes that by disciplining such students we will have solved the crisis of academic authority is grossly mistaken. Its roots, as I have shown, go much deeper.

Nor do I believe—and my judgment is somewhat tentative on this score—that we are very much nearer a solution by providing students "means to participate in the formulation and application of institutional policy affecting academic and student affairs," providing forms of due process in disciplinary proceedings, and removing all restraints on students' freedom to express themselves. These were the major recommendations of the *Joint Statement on Rights and Freedoms of Students,* issued by the Association of American Colleges, the United States National Students Association, the American Association of University Professors, and a number of other academic groups. As admirable and helpful as this statement is, and as strongly as I applaud the good judgment and diligence of those who produced it, I must conclude that it is of peripheral interest in the context of the constitutional challenge American colleges and universities presently face.

The weakness of the *Joint Statement* resides in the vagueness of the language used to define the character of the student role and in the fact that even this obscure statement was further emasculated in the resolution of endorsement by the Association of American Colleges. A "means to participate in the formulation and application of institutional policy"—the language of the *Joint Statement*—is not the same as the assurance of some form of shared control or authority over institutional policy. In fact, it might be interpreted by some as more of the "let's pretend" theory of student government, more a form of "manipulated acquiescence," than a true grant of a significant share of power.

This appearance of weakness is underscored further by the fact that the resolution of endorsement of the Association of American Colleges limits the language of the *Joint Statement* by providing that the student participation concerned—and I quote the resolution of endorsement—"may involve a variety of activities, under methods appropriate to each campus, ranging from student discussion of proposed policy in committees, in organized agencies of student government or through the student press to the more formal determination of policy by groups that include student members or, where and if delegated by appropriate authority, by groups that are composed only of students." Thus, it turns out that the colleges which endorsed the *Joint Statement* made little or no definitive commitment to the doctrine of shared power. In all probability the *Joint Statement* represents only a commitment to freedom of expression and opportunities for joint discussion; at most, it is a commitment, under some circumstances, to the joint or sole exercise by students of delegated power.

What the *Joint Statement* seems oblivious of is that the crucial issue before American colleges and universities is not due process, freedom of expression, or even forms of delegated representation, as important as these are. What is rather at issue is who shall retain ultimate control and sovereignty over the academic institution; what is at issue is whose goals, values, and objectives the college and university shall serve.

Due process in disciplinary proceedings and freedom of expression can help to assure that organs of power are responsive to the interests of those they serve. Representation on decision-making bodies whose authority is delegated by the ultimate organs of power can serve the same function even more effectively. But both of these political means fall short of reconstituting the organs of power themselves, fall short of changing the nature of ultimate sovereignty. As long as the power to be exercised by students—or faculty, for that matter—is solely delegated power rather than a share of ultimate power, the basic nature of their relationship to sovereign power remains untouched.

Thus, although the *Joint Statement* takes a significant step toward creating a more responsive academic government, it does not touch the problem of creating a more truly responsible academic government. In the long run, no institution can remain sufficiently responsive to those it serves, however well-intentioned and however well-managed, unless it is responsible to them. And it can only be responsible to them if they share, in one way or another, in the ultimate disposition and control of power. A share of delegated authority may assure responsiveness, but it is not to be confused with a share of the power to delegate authority, which is the reservoir of ultimate power. Only a share in that ultimate power can truly assure responsible government rather than merely responsive government.

In conclusion, I would urge that student activists and protectors of the old order alike have mistaken the true nature of the student revolt. The student activists do not sufficiently realize that the movement to reorganize the collegiate constitution began long before they came on the scene, that it has already progressed far beyond their wildest dreams, and that some of their tactics are inimical to its success. For their part, the protectors of the old order are mistaken about the true character of the revolt, its extent, and the kinds of remedies which are appropriate. Let us all get over our illusions and begin the difficult work of redefining the nature and character of ultimate authority in the academic world.

ILLINI BOOKS

IB-1	Grierson's Raid: A Cavalry Adventure of the Civil War	D. Alexander Brown	$1.75
IB-2	The Mars Project	Wernher von Braun	$ .95
IB-3	The New Exploration: A Philosophy of Regional Planning	Benton MacKaye, with an Introduction by Lewis Mumford	$1.75
IB-4	Tragicomedy: Its Origin and Development in Italy, France, and England	Marvin T. Herrick	$1.95
IB-5	Themes in Greek and Latin Epitaphs	Richmond Lattimore	$1.95
IB-6	The Doctrine of Responsible Party Government: Its Origins and Present State	Austin Ranney	$1.25
IB-7	An Alternative to War or Surrender	Charles E. Osgood	$1.45
IB-8	Reference Books in the Mass Media	Eleanor Blum	$1.50
IB-9	Life in a Mexican Village: Tepoztlán Restudied	Oscar Lewis	$2.95
IB-10	*Three Presidents and Their Books: The Reading of Jefferson, Lincoln, and Franklin D. Roosevelt	Arthur E. Bestor, David C. Mearns, and Jonathan Daniels	$ .95
IB-11	Cultural Sciences: Their Origin and Development	Florian Znaniecki	$2.25
IB-12	The Legend of Noah: Renaissance Rationalism in Art, Science, and Letters	Don Cameron Allen	$1.45
IB-13	*The Mathematical Theory of Communication	Claude E. Shannon and Warren Weaver	$ .95
IB-14	Philosophy and Ordinary Language	Charles E. Caton, ed.	$1.95
IB-15	Four Theories of the Press	Fred S. Siebert, Theodore Peterson, and Wilbur Schramm	$1.25
IB-16	Constitutional Problems Under Lincoln	James G. Randall	$2.95
IB-17	Viva Mexico!	Charles Macomb Flandrau, edited and with an introduction by C. Harvey Gardiner	$1.95
IB-18	Comic Theory in the Sixteenth Century	Marvin T. Herrick	$1.75

* Also available in clothbound editions.

IB-38	*Symbolic Crusade: Status Politics and the American Temperance Movement	Joseph R. Gusfield	$1.75
IB-39	*Genesis and Structure of Society	Giovanni Gentile, translated by H. S. Harris	$1.95
IB-40	The Social Philosophy of Giovanni Gentile	H. S. Harris	$2.45
IB-41	*As We Saw the Thirties: Essays on Social and Political Movements of a Decade	Rita James Simon, ed.	$2.45
IB-42	The Symbolic Uses of Politics	Murray Edelman	$2.45
IB-43	White-Collar Trade Unions: Contemporary Developments in Industrialized Societies	Adolf Sturmthal, ed.	$3.50
IB-44	*The Labor Arbitration Process	R. W. Fleming	$2.45
IB-45	*Edmund Wilson: A Study of Literary Vocation in Our Time	Sherman Paul	$2.45
IB-46	*George Santayana's America: Essays on Literature and Culture	James Ballowe, ed.	$2.25
IB-47	*The Measurement of Meaning	Charles E. Osgood, George J. Suci, and Percy H. Tannenbaum	$3.45
IB-48	*The Miracle of Growth	Foreword by Arnold Gesell	$1.75
IB-49	*Information Theory and Esthetic Perception	Abraham Moles	$2.45
IB-50	Outlawing the Spoils: A History of the Civil Service Reform Movement, 1865-1883	Ari Hoogenboom	$2.95
IB-51	*Community Colleges: A President's View	Thomas E. O'Connell	$1.95
IB-52	*The Joys and Sorrows of Recent American Art	Allen S. Weller	$3.95
IB-53	*Dimensions of Academic Freedom	Walter P. Metzger, Sanford H. Kadish, Arthur DeBardeleben, and Edward J. Bloustein	$ .95
IB-54	*Essays on Frege	E. D. Klemke, ed.	$3.95
IB-55	The Fine Hammered Steel of Herman Melville	Milton R. Stern	$2.95

* Also available in clothbound editions.

University of Illinois Press   Urbana, Chicago, and London